The Cinderella Miracle

Stage Play Script

Fairytales Happen
when angels make mistakes

Book One

The Cinderella Miracle

Stage Play Script

By
Leonard Cary

Cloud 8½ Books

Copyright © 2005 Leonard Cary Carabelos
Cover Art Copyright © 2015 Ashley Raine

All rights reserved. No part of this publication may be reproduced, stored in a retrieval system or transmitted in any form or by any means, electronic, mechanical, photocopying, recording or otherwise, without the prior written permission of the publisher. Reserved rights also include production, revision or performance for stage, motion picture, radio broadcasting, television, video or sound recording, and translation into other languages.

Stage Play Script ISBN: 978-0-9904577-2-5

Hardback ISBN: 978-0-9904577-0-1

eBook ISBN: 978-0-9904577-1-8

Published by Cloud 8½ Books, Thornton Colorado, USA

WARNING

All performances of this Work are subject to a royalty amount that must be paid whether the play is presented for profit or charity, and whether or not admission is charged. The type of organization (i.e. professional, amateur, religious, educational, etc) does not create an exemption from copyright law or royalty payment requirements. All amateur and stock performance rights to this Work are controlled exclusively by the publisher. No amateur, stock production group or individual may perform this play without securing license and royalty arrangements in advance from Cloud 8 ½ Books.

AUTHOR AND PUBLISHER CREDIT

All organizations receiving permission to produce this play must give author and publisher credit in any and all advertisements, publicity and programs relating to its production. The author's billing, "By Leonard Cary", must appear directly below the play title on a separate line where no other written matter appears. Advertisements and publicity must also include the publisher billing "Produced by special arrangement with Cloud 8 ½ Books" in any location provided that it is still reasonably associated with the play title.

ADDITIONAL RESOURCES

PRODUCTION KIT

The *Production Kit* provides resources for scaling the script, staging suggestions, music & sound effect MP3s, magic trick details and technical materials created especially for this show. Look for the Production Kit page at the end of this script for more information.

CHAPTER BOOK

Producers, directors and lead actors can gain a deeper understanding of character traits, character development and setting details by reading *The Cinderella Miracle* in the illustrated children's chapter book version. The book is available on Amazon, Barnes and Noble, and other websites where books are sold.

CAST OF CHARACTERS
In order of appearance

MR RICHARDSON: A department manager in Heaven. A stickler for forms and procedures, but soft hearted underneath.

CLARA: Cinderella's guardian angel (a.k.a. fairy godmother). A bit scatter-brained.

CINDERELLA: Beautiful, sweet, and kind. "Ella Ashton" is her given name.

THEODORE THE MOUSE: References to THEODORE are for the actor playing a mouse turned into a coachman. References to THEODORE THE MOUSE indicate a stick or finger puppet on the fireplace mantle.

ELINORA: A stepsister of Cinderella. Beautiful or not doesn't matter, it's all in the ugly attitude.

MARGARET: Older and smarter sister of Elinora, with similar attitude.

STEPMOTHER: The cruel stepmother of Cinderella. "Evelyn Ashton", widow of James Ashton.

CAPTAIN: An officer in the king's military. His uniform includes a sash from shoulder to hip that Prince Henry takes in Scene 8.

ROYAL PAGE: The king's messenger and crier.

JAMES: James Ashton, Cinderella's deceased father. *Not* to be played as a ghost with a pale face, etc.

THEODORE: Cinderella's furry mouse friend after being transformed into her carriage coachman.

PRINCE: His majesty, Prince Henry the Third.

KING: His majesty, King Henry the Second.

QUEEN: Her majesty, the Queen.

NICHOLAS: Prince Henry's personal attendant and friend.

GUINEVERE: The lady Guinevere Needham. An eligible young lady attending the ball.

CASSANDRA: The lady Cassandra Wakefield. Another young lady at the ball.

MAIDENS: Optional dialog shared between additional ladies who are guests at the ball.

SCENES

Scene 1: *Forms and Procedures*
Mr. Richardson's office, early morning, long ago

Scene 2: *A Typical Morning*
Stepmother's kitchen, the same morning

Scene 3: *The Impact Report*
Mr. Richardson's office, a moment later

Scene 4: *By Royal Decree*
Stepmother's kitchen, a little later

Scene 5: *Dangerous Tactics*
Mr. Richardson's office, a moment later

Scene 6: *Of Mice and Magic*
Stepmother's kitchen, early evening

Scene 7: *Mission Accomplished*
Mr. Richardson's office, the same evening

Scene 8: *Blind Ambition*
The Royal Palace Ballroom, 8:00 pm

Scene 9: *A Breath of Fresh Air*
At the Royal Garden Footbridge, nearly 10:00 pm

Scene 10: *Belle of the Ball*
The Royal Palace Ballroom, after 11:00 pm

Scene 11: *Coincidental Moments*
At the Royal Garden Footbridge, just before midnight

Scene 12: *Tactical Errors*
Balcony Seating, moments later

Scene 13: *Passion and Purpose*
The Royal Palace Ballroom, 12:10 am

Scene 14: *Emergency Mission*
Balcony Seating, moments later

Scene 15: *Revelation and Redemption*
Stepmother's kitchen, 1:30 am

Scene 16: *Ripples and Waves*
Mr. Richardson's office, a moment later

Scene 17: *Heaven Blessed*
The Royal Palace Ballroom, 3:00 pm

SETTINGS
In order of initial occurrence

Underlined items are basic required elements in each setting.

SETTING: The Department of Minor Miracles and Blessings

Mr. Richardson's office in the clouds of heaven. Majestic clouds float over blue sky walls with rays of sunlight shining through. The set pieces have a 1950's style with a wooden <u>office desk</u>, <u>two chairs</u> (one behind and one in front of the desk) and a four-drawer <u>filing cabinet</u>. On the desktop is a <u>telephone</u> and a stacked pair of in/out boxes. On top of the filing cabinet is a long 3 x 5 <u>index card box</u>. A sign "Department of Minor Miracles and Blessings" may appear in the office, or painted on the office door with "Richardson" underneath. The setting is best as a separately curtained area off of the main stage so that its scenes can continue while other scene changes occur. If a separately curtained area is not available then consider the "Cloud 8 ½" setting may help speed up a few scene changes.

SETTING: Stepmother's Kitchen

A 16th century rustic kitchen with stone walls a <u>fireplace</u> and mantle. Set pieces include a wooden <u>table and chairs</u>, a <u>wicker basket of laundry</u>, <u>a broom</u> and other basic rustic kitchen items. There are three real or implied exits; a "hallway" (closest to the fireplace) leads to the rest of the house, a "kitchen door" leads "outside" and a "hidden gap" between the fireplace and an upstage wall for the spiritual/magical entrances of JAMES, CLARA and THEODORE which may include smoke or lighting effects.

SETTING: The Royal Palace Ballroom

Stone walls of a 16th century castle are dressed in fine linen drapes. A large majestic clock is upstage center. Two ornate thrones are upstage right, preferably on a raised platform. The thrones and platform may be removed for Scene 17. The main entrance is the stage left wing. A secondary "hidden" entrance may be up center (hidden by the clock) or center right for JAMES' entrance in Scene 8.

SETTING: The Royal Garden Footbridge

A small, arched 16th century footbridge traverses a narrow creek that divides lush green royal gardens from the palace grounds. Acting space to the left and right of a small bridge should be available with the most space stage left which suggests the wide open gardens. The right wing is therefore an exit back toward the palace. However, Cinderella's entrance via the garden and her run back out through the garden at midnight (followed by Theodore and Nicholas) are best played up a house right aisle.

SETTING: Cloud 8 ½ (optional)

A small white cloud with two theater-style chairs and a small "Cloud 8 ½" sign at the foot of the chairs. The setting is optional depending on the venue. These two scenes could also be played in "The Department of Minor Miracles and Blessings". Theater box seats at the side of the house can be a good setting if available.

The Cinderella Miracle
by Leonard Cary

SCENE 1

Forms and Procedures

Mr. Richardson's Office, early morning, long ago.

SETTING: The Department of Minor Miracles and Blessings

AT RISE: MR RICHARDSON sits behind his desk. He is writing with a shiny gold pen on a pad of paper.

SFX: There is a knock at the door.

MR RICHARDSON: Enter.
CLARA: *(Entering)* Mr. Richardson, sir, may I have a moment of your time?
MR RICHARDSON: *(Stands to shake her hand)* Yes, what can I do for you Miss...?
CLARA: My name is Clara.
MR RICHARDSON: Nice to meet you, Clara.
CLARA: Oh, thank you, it's very nice to meet you, sir. I've heard so many wonderful things about this department. Your reputation precedes you, Mr. Richardson.
MR RICHARDSON: Thank you. And your business today is?
CLARA: I was hoping you could help me with my current assignment. Her name is Cinderella.
MR RICHARDSON: Cinderella.

(He opens a file drawer, starts searching. Optional effect: The file drawer opens on its own.)

CLARA: She's a wonderful girl. I've been looking after her... well... since a little before her father passed away. He is a very sweet man-
MR RICHARDSON: Is that spelled C-I...
CLARA: C-I-N-D-E-R-E-L-L-A
MR RICHARDSON: *(Continuing his search)* C...CI...

CLARA: James. That's Cinderella's father's name...James Ashton. He died...let's see...I believe it would be almost ten years ago he passed away. I should mention that he recently visited his daughter.

MR RICHARDSON: *(Stopping his search.)* I beg your pardon?!

CLARA: Oh, I know it is irregular-

MR RICHARDSON: Highly irregular! The spiritual presence of the dearly departed usually only makes things more difficult for their loved ones to move forward!

CLARA: Yes, I know. I did ask him about it. He said he's on special assignment. You wouldn't know anything about that, would you?

MR RICHARDSON: He's not on assignment from my department, perhaps The Department of Redemption?

CLARA: Oh, I wouldn't think that would be needed, not for Cinderella. *(Pause.)* Should I be concerned about him?

MR RICHARDSON: No, Clara. I'm sure Mr. Ashton's assignment has been approved, and most likely- *(Pointing up.)* from the top.

CLARA: *(Looks up.)* Oh my, yes of course.

MR RICHARDSON: *(Returns to searching.)* And you would have been informed if any coordination efforts were needed.

CLARA: I suppose so. *(Pause.)* Mr. Richardson, has your department ever used a dearly departed on a special mission?

MR RICHARDSON: No, the Department of Minor Miracles and Blessings only dispatches <u>angels</u> on assignment.

CLARA: I'm still not a true angel.

MR RICHARDSON: Clara, the wings do not make the angel. I don't even wear mine most of the time.

CLARA: Oh, but I've always wanted a pair, Mr. Richardson. They're so grand, and you can get about so much faster.

MR RICHARDSON: Patience, Clara. It usually doesn't take more than a few decades of fieldwork to earn them.

CLARA: Yes, I know.

MR RICHARDSON: Does Cinderella go by some other name?

CLARA: Oh, I'm sorry. Cinderella is a nickname her stepsisters gave her because she sleeps on the fireplace hearth and is often dirty from the cinders.

MR RICHARDSON: Then her given name would be?

CLARA: Her father named her Ella, Ella Ashton.

MR RICHARDSON: *(Searching the files again. Possibly a different drawer.)* Ella.

CLARA: I'm sure they were trying to hurt her feelings when they first called her Cinderella. But she understands how important it is to serve so she's adopted the name and wears it like a medal of honor. They do treat her very poorly though. More like a slave than a servant.

MR RICHARDSON: I'm sorry, who treats her poorly?

CLARA: Do forgive me, I'm just rambling on. I was referring to Cinderella's stepsisters. They are so cruel to her. But her stepmother is really the cause of it all.

MR RICHARDSON: *(Pulling a thin file folder out of the drawer.)* There she is. *(Opens it and looks at the 2 pieces of paper inside.)* Well, Clara, there's not much here.

CLARA: No?

MR RICHARDSON: In fact, none of the required reports.

CLARA: Required reports?

MR RICHARDSON: Clara, I cannot grant a minor miracle or a blessing without all the necessary paperwork.

CLARA: Oh...well if it's just a few pieces of paper you need—

MR RICHARDSON: *(He sits and starts pulling forms out of a desk drawer and organizing them on his desktop.)* A Needs Analysis Form, Prayer Life Report, Servant Walk Report, Miracle and Blessing Impact Form, and a Coincidence Coordination Opportunities Form.

CLARA: Oh my.

MR RICHARDSON: You'll need to study the subject in detail—

CLARA: The subject?

MR RICHARDSON: Ella — or Cinderella — your subject. There's a great deal of research work needed to complete some of these, especially the MBI and CCO forms.

CLARA: MBI?

MR RICHARDSON: Miracle and Blessing Impact Form. *(Finally stopping to look CLARA in the eye.)* Madam, if you don't mind my saying so, you look a bit distressed.

CLARA: I feel a bit distressed.

MR RICHARDSON: *(Handing her the forms)* Take these with you and work on them a little each day.

CLARA: But Cinderella needs my help now. She's at that age, Mr. Richardson, when your heart needs to know love or it might be broken forever.

MR RICHARDSON: *(Pauses then takes the stack of forms back and puts them on a clipboard)* Alright. Let's see if I can help you get started. *(Reading from the form)* Needs Analysis Form, section A: Describe the miracle or blessing being requested. Please include projected dates and times.

CLARA: Well, she needs to get out more and meet new people. She has no friends and her stepsisters-

MR RICHARDSON: Needs to get out more? You'll need to be more specific.

CLARA: Well, for example, occasionally there are special events at the palace or in the town square. If she could go to something like that, maybe she would make new friends!

MR RICHARDSON: You want a Minor Miracle to send a young girl to party?

CLARA: It doesn't sound very good when you put it that way.

MR RICHARDSON: No, it does not.

CLARA: Mr. Richardson, if you could just see her situation you would understand.

MR RICHARDSON: It is not my job to study the subject. That is your job, and then you give me the summarized information *on the required forms*!

CLARA: Please don't yell at me.

MR RICHARDSON: My apologies. Let's try a different form. Perhaps the Prayer Life Report or the Servant Walk Report?

CLARA: And what are those?

MR RICHARDSON: The Prayer Life Report describes the subject's efforts to communicate with God, while the Servant Walk Report details her efforts to live according to God's plan.

CLARA: Oh, yes! Those are easy. You just need to see her for a few minutes!

MR RICHARDSON: *(Tries to hand the clipboard to CLARA but she doesn't take it.)* Just fill in the information in section-

CLARA: *(Stands up, moves to the edge of the office and looks down to earth)* Right over here. She should be waking up in just a moment!

MR RICHARDSON: The form, Madam.

CLARA: Please come here and watch. It will only take a *minute* of your time!

MR RICHARDSON: *(Standing and crossing next to CLARA)* Very well.

SLOW FADE TO BLACK

SCENE 2

A Typical Morning

Stepmother's Kitchen, the same morning.

SETTING: Stepmother's Kitchen

AT RISE: A basket of fruit and a loaf of bread sit on the kitchen table. Cinderella is lying on the fireplace hearth under a thin blanket.

(THEODORE THE MOUSE pokes his head out of his mouse hole at the corner of the fireplace mantle.)

[Start of optional offstage dialog section. The following dialog may be used if the production has sufficient lighting resources of the "spinning like a tornado" effect mentioned later.]

CLARA (O.S.): There she is.

MR RICHARDSON (O.S.): That little child curled up on the floor?

CLARA (O.S.): Yes, that's where she sleeps most nights. Her stepmother won't spend the money on a bed, and Cinderella is not allowed to touch the good linens or blankets either. That is, except to wash them, of course. *(Pauses. Thoughtfully.)* Wash them...Oh my!

(Bright and tight spotlighting create a "spinning like a tornado" and may even accent the items in the following line.)

CLARA (O.S.): Laundry clean... cellar door closed and locked... dishes done... shelves dusted... chairs and kitchen table...

MR RICHARDSON (O.S.): Madam, what are you doing?!

(Tornado spotlighting stops with one light left on the loaf of bread.)

CLARA (O.S.): Oh! Mr. Richardson, I'm sorry. I forgot we were sharing the same sight. I thought I was actually in the room with her!

MR RICHARDSON (O.S.): Please, just give me a little warning next time you want to spin the room around like a tornado!

CLARA (O.S.): Oh dear, she left the bread out!

MR RICHARDSON (O.S.): I beg your pardon?

CLARA (O.S.): The loaf of fresh bread on the table; she left it out to cool last night and forgot to put it away. If it's the least bit stale, then she will pay a dear price!

MR RICHARDSON (O.S.): For stale bread?

CLARA (O.S.): Oh, most certainly.

MR RICHARDSON (O.S.): Well, I'm surprised the mice didn't eat the entire loaf down to crumbs.

CLARA (O.S.): Mice? What mice?

(Spotlighting cross fades from the bread to THEODORE THE MOUSE.)

MR RICHARDSON (O.S.): There's one right there. And where you see one mouse, you can be sure there are hundreds more hiding.

CLARA (O.S.): Oh, that's not a mouse. It's Theodore!

MR RICHARDSON (O.S.): I assure you, Clara, I know what mice look like, and that is a mouse.

CLARA (O.S.): Well, yes, of course it is a mouse. But that's Theodore, Cinderella's little friend.

MR RICHARDSON (O.S.): You mean her...pet.

CLARA (O.S.): I know what I mean, Mr. Richardson. Theodore is her friend, and there aren't any other mice around either. There are plenty of cats outside to see to that.

(CINDERELLA has been waking up during the last part of the above.)

[End of optional offstage dialog section]

CINDERELLA: *(She stands, yawns, stretches and begins to fold her blanket.)* Good morning, Theodore. Did you sleep well? It got a bit chilly last night, didn't it? *(Scratching his ear with her index finger.)* I'll bet you're hungry already. But we mustn't forget our morning prayers come first. *(Hands together and closing her eyes.)* Dear Lord, thank you for another beautiful morning. Please bless my stepsisters and stepmother today with the joy of Your spirit. Help me to take care of their needs with patience, and to be a reminder to them of You and Your grace. Amen. *(She opens her eyes and looks at THEODORE.)* And Lord, please help Theodore to stay safely out of sight and out from underfoot. Amen.

(CINDERELLA brushes cinders off her clothes and onto the hearth then puts her folded blanket away. She stares for a moment at the loaf of bread and breathes out a sigh, then breaks a small corner off and brings it to THEODORE THE MOUSE.)

CINDERELLA: Here you are, Theodore. Now don't eat it too quickly; you might upset your tummy.

(THEODORE THE MOUSE disappears back into his hole. CINDERELLA begins sweeping the ash on the hearth back into the fireplace.)

ELINORA (O.S.): *(Yelling)* Cinderella, where is my blue dress?
CINDERELLA: Just a moment, Elinora, I'll find it for you.
MARGARET (O.S.): *(Also yelling)* Cinderella, I'm hungry! Have you started breakfast?
CINDERELLA: I was just going to get a fire started, Margaret. Can I bring you some bread and jam?
ELINORA (O.S.): I called her first! I want my dress!
MARGARET (O.S.): I can't wait! I'm lying here wasting away. Bring the bread and jam immediately!
ELINORA (O.S.): Mother!
STEPMOTHER (O.S.): Girls, please don't squabble. Cinderella will take care of you both. *(Yelling)* Cinderella!
CINDERELLA: Yes, Stepmother.

STEPMOTHER (O.S.): Bring me my slippers.
CINDERELLA: *(Exiting via the hallway)* Yes, Stepmother.

BLACKOUT

SCENE 3

The Impact Report

Mr. Richardson's Office, a moment later.

SETTING: The Department of Minor Miracles and Blessings

AT RISE: CLARA and MR RICHARDSON are in their prior positions, looking down to Earth.

CLARA: Everyday the same thing. Cinderella's stepsisters are so cruel.

MR RICHARDSON: *(Angrily)* Everyday?

CLARA: And they're just getting started.

MR RICHARDSON: She prays for them every morning?

CLARA: Every morning.

MR RICHARDSON: And submits herself to being their servant in her own home?

CLARA: Continuously.

MR RICHARDSON: How does she tolerate them? *(Raising his arm in a backhanded motion to strike.)* I mean I would just-

CLARA: Mr. Richardson!

MR RICHARDSON: Oh. My apologies, madam.

CLARA: I believe that example should satisfy your paperwork.

MR RICHARDSON: *(Returning to his desk, he picks up the clipboard and fills in some details.)* Well, let's see. Needs Analysis..."yes...no...no...two evil stepsisters and a cruel stepmother". Very good. *(Flips the page.)* Prayer Life Report...hmmm...yes "every morning". What about other times?

(MR RICHARDSON takes notes as CLARA answers.)

CLARA: Oh she prays at every meal. Silently, of course, because her stepmother doesn't let her speak at the table. And every night before bed...and really just about every chance she gets.

MR RICHARDSON: Excellent. *(He writes a little more then flips to the next form on his clipboard.)* Servant Walk Report...I think I might need extra paper.

CLARA: Maybe you should just summarize.

MR RICHARDSON: Right. *(He makes a few notes and flips a page.)* Okay, now the MBI form.

CLARA: That was the one you said would require research?

MR RICHARDSON: Yes, let me explain.

CLARA: Please do.

MR RICHARDSON: The impact form is where you document how the Miracle or Blessing will change lives. Not just the receiver's life but the other lives he or she comes in contact with now and in the future. Section B is a description of the impact and how it relates to God's plan for salvation.

CLARA: My goodness, that sounds like an important form.

MR RICHARDSON: It is, Clara. The minimum report requirements are to cover the impact to lives for the next one hundred years.

CLARA: One hundred years! I have to research how a change in Cinderella's life will ripple through other lives over the next one hundred years?!

MR RICHARDSON: Yes, Clara, but it's not as difficult as it sounds. *(Puts down the clipboard and picks up CINDERELLA'S file folder.)* Let's see if I can find an example.

CLARA: That might help.

MR RICHARDSON: *(Scans the two pages in CINDERELLA'S file folder.)* Here we are. She has a marriage reference number.

CLARA: Oh, that's marvelous! Cinderella will make a wonderful wife.

MR RICHARDSON: *(He goes to the 3 x 5 card file, open's it and starts searching. Optional: the card box may magically float to him or open for him.)* She <u>might</u> make a wonderful wife. The marriage reference is only a possibility, not a guarantee.

CLARA: Oh, I wish it could be a guarantee. Love is exactly what she needs.

MR RICHARDSON: *(Pulling a card out of the box.)* Here it is. Ella will marry-

CLARA: What? What does it say?

MR RICHARDSON: Prince Henry.

CLARA: The *prince*? My Cinderella could marry the *prince*?!

MR RICHARDSON: *(Opens a file drawer and starts searching.)* That is what the card says.

CLARA: That's wonderful...you see? Cinderella does need a miracle! She's never even met the prince, she doesn't know anyone! Her stepmother keeps her working all the time. She never leaves home.

MR RICHARDSON: *(Pulling a file folder out that is stuffed thick with paper.)* Prince Henry.

CLARA: My goodness!

MR RICHARDSON: *(Very quickly flipping through pages, scanning the information at an impossibly fast rate.)* Royalty often has a significant impact...and a thick file.

CLARA: But he's just a prince. He hasn't done anything yet. He's not the king.

MR RICHARDSON: With or without Cinderella, he will be king someday. Here we are. Ten years after his father passes away, Prince Henry will go to war with another kingdom, but... *(Very quickly flips through several more pages.)* if he marries Cinderella...there will be a peaceful resolution. Ten thousand lives will be spared because of her influence in his life!

CLARA: Ten thousand!

MR RICHARDSON: *(Referring to another page.)* Together they will have seven children and thirty-two grandchildren.

CLARA: Seven children, oh how lovely! She will be such a wonderful mother.

MR RICHARDSON: If we cross reference the children and grandchildren, and the lives saved from war, and their children and grandchildren, we could trace the rippling effect that a miracle will have over time.

CLARA: I never imagined a minor miracle could be so powerful.

MR RICHARDSON: God's plans are always executed through miracles and the ripples they create.

CLARA: Is there any way to tell when Cinderella and the prince will meet? When they might be married?

MR RICHARDSON: True love can be tricky. Sometimes there's only one chance for two hearts to come together, and in other cases there may be many chances. But either way, the marriage reference always has a last opportunity date, a point in time when the two must finally join in marriage, or their paths will separate forever. *(Picking up and looking at the 3 x 5 index card.)* The latest possible wedding date is... tomorrow!

CLARA: Tomorrow?! How is that even possible?

MR RICHARDSON: *(Picks up the clipboard again, flips through several pages and starts writing again. In a bit of a panic.)* And you say Cinderella has never met the prince?

CLARA: No! Never! The only friend she has is that mouse. *(Getting impatient.)* Don't you think those forms could wait? We need to do something immediately!

MR RICHARDSON: I'm just completing the Miracle and Blessing Impact Form. Obviously, the impact in this case is enormous!

CLARA: So, you'll grant Cinderella a miracle?

MR RICHARDSON: Yes, Clara, we just need to figure out how to get Cinderella and the prince to meet...and in the next twenty-four hours.

SFX: Herald trumpets and Horse hooves (continuing through the scene change)

CLARA: *(Moving to the edge of the set and looking down to Earth)* Oh my, it must be something important. *(Pulling MR RICHARDSON toward her)* Come look.

SLOW FADE TO BLACK

SCENE 4

By Royal Decree

Stepmother's Kitchen, a little later

SETTING: Stepmother's Kitchen. The scene 2 bread and fruit basket have been replaced with a slender copper pitcher on the table filled with wildflowers.

AT RISE: Lighting comes up full and STEPMOTHER enters from the hallway, crossing to the kitchen door.

SFX: Herald trumpet and horse hooves (continuing for a few moments from the previous scene)

STEPMOTHER: *(Looking out a window by the kitchen door.)* Oh! The royal guard! Girls! Girls, come quickly. There are men here from the royal guard!
MARGARET: *(Entering from the hallway and crossing to the kitchen door.)* Men! Oh Mother, are they here for me?
STEPMOTHER: Perhaps they are here to arrest you.
MARGARET: Mother!
STEPMOTHER: Just a little jest, my darling Margaret.
ELINORA: *(Entering from the hallway.)* Have I missed anything?
MARGARET: Don't you always miss everything, Elinora?
ELINORA: Mother, she's being mean to me again!
STEPMOTHER: Girls, behave yourselves! Try not to embarrass me.
MARGARET AND ELINORA: Yes, mother.

(CINDERELLA quietly enters from the hallway.)

SFX: A knock at the door

STEPMOTHER: You may enter.
CAPTAIN: *(Stiffly entering with sword drawn at his shoulder in military procession style. Stands at attention throughout.)* A message from King Henry the Second.

ROYAL PAGE: *(Entering and reading from an official scroll.)* Hear ye, citizens of the realm, an urgent message from His Majesty, King Henry the Second, regarding the marital status of his son, Prince Henry the Third.

STEPMOTHER: Marital status?

ROYAL PAGE: By royal decree, the prince has been commanded to seek, select and marry a maiden before the full moon has waned, fifteen days hence.

ELINORA: Fifteen days?!

STEPMOTHER: Quiet, Elinora!

ROYAL PAGE: Your king and queen do hereby cordially command that all eligible ladies shall attend a grand ball this very evening. The prince shall meet every attending maiden with the intention of selecting a young lady to be the kingdom's new princess, and our future queen.

MARGARET: It's tonight, Mother!

ELINORA: What will I wear?

MARGARET: You? What does it matter? The prince would never even consider-

ELINORA: I have just as much a chance as you.

MARGARET: Huh!

ELINORA: More. I'm younger and far prettier. You're practically an old maid.

MARGARET: *(Threateningly approaching ELINORA.)* You take that back!

STEPMOTHER: Girls, please! Your manners.

MARGARET AND ELINORA: Yes, mother.

STEPMOTHER: *(Crossing to the ROYAL PAGE.)* Might I ask, what has prompted the urgency of the king's decree?

ROYAL PAGE: *(Very informally, in a gossiping tone.)* The prince and his father had a bit of a fight.

CAPTAIN: *(Still at attention.)* Ah-Ahem!

ROYAL PAGE: If Prince Henry fails to act in accordance with the decree, the king will select a bride for him.

STEPMOTHER: And if he refuses to marry?

ROYAL PAGE: He will be thrown into the dun-

(The CAPTAIN has marched toward the ROYAL PAGE and threateningly brought down his sword to strike the floor.)

ROYAL PAGE: *(With a squeaky voice)* Yes, Captain?

STEPMOTHER: *(To MARGARET and ELINORA)* The prince is being forced to take a bride. How marvelous.

CINDERELLA: Marvelous? It's dreadfully wrong.

STEPMOTHER: Hold your tongue, Cinderella!

CAPTAIN: *(Threateningly to the ROYAL PAGE.)* I fear we may have overstayed our welcome.

ROYAL PAGE: Of course...we must take our leave now. Good day to you, ladies.

STEPMOTHER: And a good day to you...and thank you.

(The ROYAL PAGE exits followed by the CAPTAIN. The instant they are out of sight MARGARET and ELINORA scream with delight. STEPMOTHER smiles broadly. CINDERELLA shakes her head sadly.)

STEPMOTHER: Girls, girls we have much to do to get ready.

MARGARET AND ELINORA: Yes, Mother!

CINDERELLA: Stepmother?

STEPMOTHER: What do you want, Cinderella?

CINDERELLA: I was wondering...if I could go to the ball.

MARGARET: You?

ELINORA: That's ridiculous!

STEPMOTHER: Really, Cinderella, don't you think you've embarrassed me enough? Speaking out of turn with the captain of the royal guard and the king's royal page listening to every disgraceful word. They must think I've raised you to be the village idiot. You saw how quickly they left after your foolish remark.

CINDERELLA: I'm very sorry, Stepmother.

STEPMOTHER: As you should be.

CINDERELLA: But the decree did command that all eligible ladies attend.

STEPMOTHER: Indeed, it did. *(Pausing to scheme)* Very well, Cinderella. You may go to the ball.

CINDERELLA: Oh, thank you!

MARGARET: Mother!

ELINORA: She can't-

STEPMOTHER: Quiet! *(Wickedly sweet)* However, you must finish all your chores. Certainly, even the king must understand that duty and responsibility come before dancing and music. Don't you agree, Cinderella?

CINDERELLA: Yes, stepmother.

STEPMOTHER: And you will help your stepsisters prepare for the ball.

CINDERELLA: But-

STEPMOTHER: That is your punishment for embarrassing me in front of the royal guard.

CINDERELLA: Yes, Stepmother.

STEPMOTHER: And...you will sweep all the floors, and wash the windows, the drapes and the linens.

CINDERELLA: But...begging your pardon, Stepmother...but why would all those things need to be done today of all days?

STEPMOTHER: Darling girl, I am certain that either Margaret, or Elinora...or you, my dear...will capture the prince's heart tonight. And then he is certain to visit the home of his bride to be. We wouldn't want royalty in a dirty house now, would we?

CINDERELLA: *(Hanging her head in defeat.)* No, Stepmother.

STEPMOTHER: We're in agreement then.

MARGARET: Mother, I need Cinderella first. My best dress has a tear in the hem.

ELINORA: No, Mother, that's not fair! Margaret knows my hair must be brushed two hundred times.

(THEODORE THE MOUSE comes out of his hole and starts running back and forth on the fireplace mantle.)

CINDERELLA: *(Pretending to be frightened.)* Oh my, it's a mouse!

(MARGARET and ELINORA scream and run out the hallway exit.)

STEPMOTHER: *(Crossing to the hallway exit.)* And Cinderella-

CINDERELLA: Yes, Stepmother?

STEPMOTHER: *(Just before she exits)* Kill that mouse.

CINDERELLA: *(Crosses to the fireplace mantle.)* Thank you, Theodore. *(She picks up the broom and begins sweeping, stops and sadly sits in a kitchen chair holding back tears.)* Father, I wish you were here. I wish you could be with me... to tell me what I'm doing wrong.

(THEODORE THE MOUSE exit via his hole. JAMES, CINDERELLA's deceased father, appears from the gap at the fireplace wall. CINDERELLA's conversation is with herself. She cannot see or hear JAMES.)

JAMES: Ella, I'm here. I know it is difficult.

CINDERELLA: I've tried to remember what you taught me about kindness and forgiveness.

JAMES: I'm counting on you, Ella. You must stay strong.

CINDERELLA: I pray, and I am thankful.

JAMES: Your stepmother hasn't always been this way. I remember a different woman.

CINDERELLA: *(Beginning to breakdown.)* Why? Why do they hate me so?

JAMES: They've done it for so long, it's all they know.

CINDERELLA: Father, I try to love them, but they hate me.

JAMES: Don't lose hope, my sweet Ella. I need you to keep trying. Things will work out, but you must continue to respond to them with love.

CINDERELLA: Is being loved just a childhood dream? I haven't felt loved...since you left me, Father.

(CINDERELLA puts her face into her hands and cries.)

JAMES: You are loved, Ella. Love isn't a childhood dream. You get to take it with you. Everything else stays behind when you leave, especially the tears. But all the times you have loved...you get to keep every bit of it...because it is the love that is real.

SLOW FADE TO BLACK

SCENE 5

Dangerous Tactics

Mr. Richardson's Office, a moment later.

SETTING: The Department of Minor Miracles and Blessings

AT RISE: CLARA and MR RICHARDSON are in their last positions, looking down to earth. MR RICHARDSON's face is in a tight trying-to-hold-back-tears expression. CLARA is gently dabbing her cheeks with a handkerchief and sniffling loudly.

CLARA: Oh, the poor dear... *(Blows her nose into the handkerchief.)* I'm afraid her heart is truly broken now. Is there any way to help her?

MR RICHARDSON: *(With a crack in his voice.)* Yes... *(Clears his throat, with more conviction)* Yes, Clara, it is never too late for a miracle.

CLARA: Really?

MR RICHARDSON: We simply need to find the right coincidence.

CLARA: The right coincidence?

MR RICHARDSON: Yes, coincidence...the mechanism of minor miracles. You do know my official title, don't you?

CLARA: Oh, um...no, Mr. Richardson, I'm afraid I don't. I do apologize.

MR RICHARDSON: No apology needed. My official title is "Manager of Coincidence Coordination".

CLARA: Coincidence Coordination?

MR RICHARDSON: Exactly.

CLARA: But a coincidence is a fluke, a chance happening, a random event. How can it be *coordinated*?

MR RICHARDSON: When I do my job right, coincidence is exactly what a minor miracle...looks like.

CLARA: So you cause miracles to occur by coordinating events...

MR RICHARDSON: ...that would normally occur at random...

CLARA: ...so that a person's life is blessed with a miracle, but it looks like an uncommon coincidence.

MR RICHARDSON: Very good, Clara.

CLARA: Are there any coincidences that are just that...a coincidence?

MR RICHARDSON: Certainly. But there are far more unrecognized miracles and blessings.

CLARA: But, wouldn't more people believe in God if miracles were more obvious? If they weren't so easily dismissed as coincidence?

MR RICHARDSON: That is another misconception. Miracles are not made so that people can have faith in God. Quite the opposite. Faith in God is how you see the miracle provided through a coincidence. The true purpose of a miracle is to advance God's purposes and spread His love.

CLARA: I think I understand.

MR RICHARDSON: *(Flipping to the last page on the clipboard.)* Good, now that brings us to the Coincidence Coordination Opportunities Form.

CLARA: Oh my, do we really have time for that?

MR RICHARDSON: *(Opening CINDERELLA's thin file folder)* Of course. We just need to look for opportunities in Cinderella's file. *(Picks up the individual pages one at a time and gives CLARA a patronizing look.)* But, there's not much here.

CLARA: *(Embarrassed)* No, there isn't.

MR RICHARDSON: No friends? Distant family?

CLARA: She works in the house from sunup to sundown. She's not allowed off the estate. I wonder, really, if there is anyone at all.

MR RICHARDSON: *(Opening the PRINCE's thick file folder.)* Perhaps there will be clues in Prince Henry's file. If they marry, then some event in his future could connect to an opportunity in Cinderella's life that we can use.

(MR RICHARDSON stares intently into the stack of papers as he fans them in a turbo charged speed read.)

CLARA: Anything?

MR RICHARDSON: *(Pause)* Unfortunately, nothing that will help get her to the ball. I am afraid we will need to take the direct approach. It is a bit unusual, and quite dangerous.

CLARA: Dangerous?!

MR RICHARDSON: Yes, Clara...dangerous. You will need to bestow a direct blessing on Cinderella without the use of coincidence.

CLARA: Why is that dangerous?

MR RICHARDSON: Because direct miracles and blessings look to the world, like magic.

CLARA: Oh my! Magic! That's not good.

MR RICHARDSON: No, it is not. Magic is always self serving while miracles serve God's purpose. Those who see the truth will know that God's purpose is the end result, but the things you will do for Cinderella will look like magic to those who are blinded by the world. We must, therefore, do everything we can to make your work look trivial and unattainable so that people have no desire to pursue magical powers for themselves.

(MR RICHARDSON produces a fairy godmother magic wand.)

CLARA: A wand?

MR RICHARDSON: Yes. You will visit Cinderella and give her what she needs using this wand. You are no longer her Guardian Angel.

CLARA: I'm not?

MR RICHARDSON: You are now Cinderella's... *(With a "Fairy Godmother" voice and gesture)* "Fairy Godmother".

CLARA: Won't that be fun?!

MR RICHARDSON: *(With one hand he starts typing on the edge of the wand like a keyboard.)* Now, in addition to calling yourself *Fairy Godmother* you must make it clear that your *magic* will expire.

CLARA: Expire?

MR RICHARDSON: *(Handing the wand to her.)* I've set it expire at midnight. Anything you transform with this wand will turn back to its original form at the stroke of midnight.

CLARA: Is that really necessary?

MR RICHARDSON: It is just another safety precaution that must be taken when a minor miracle is bestowed without the use of a coincidence.

CLARA : I think I understand...No I don't. How does all of this help?!

MR RICHARDSON: If you are called "Fairy Godmother" and wave a magic wand with temporary effects, then the strange things you do will be dismissed...

CLARA: ...as childhood imagination rather than self serving magic.

MR RICHARDSON: Yes, and God's plan will be the end result. Which reminds me...the most important form of all. *(Pulls another form from his desk drawer.)* The Miracle Request and Approval Form.

CLARA: But you already approved it.

MR RICHARDSON: *(Quickly filling in the form as he talks.)* No, Clara, I compile the research, plan out options and submit requests. There's only one person who can approve a miracle. He just needs to put his initials on this form. *(Turning the page toward her and handing her the pen.)* Sign here please.

CLARA: How long will that take?

MR RICHARDSON: Only a moment.

(Stage magic or special effects may be used to transform the paper, or fly it up to the sky and drop it back down into MR RICHARDSONs hand, etc. See the Production Kit for trick suggestions.)

MR RICHARDSON: *(He holds the form up for CLARA to see.)* It looks like you have work to do.

CLARA: *(Smiling as she reads initials now on the form)* J. C.

SLOW FADE TO BLACK

SCENE 6

Of Mice and Magic

Stepmother's Kitchen, early evening.

SETTING: Stepmother's Kitchen. The pitcher of wildflowers has been removed. A basket of clothing and linens sits on the floor by the table.

AT RISE: STEPMOTHER, MARGARET and ELINORA are now in formal ball gowns. CINDERELLA sits on her knees putting the final stitches in the hem of MARGARET's gown. A pair of scissors rests on the floor.

ELINORA: Hurry up, Cinderella. We're going to be late.

MARGARET: She's been pouting and moving like a snail all afternoon.

STEPMOTHER: Really, Cinderella, you have been rather depressing on this festive day.

CINDERELLA: I'm very sorry, Stepmother.

MARGARET: *(Seeing CINDERELLA finishing.)* Is that it?

CINDERELLA: *(Cutting the tail of thread with the scissors.)* Yes, it's done.

MARGARET: *(Spinning around.)* Mother, how do I look?

STEPMOTHER: Quite lovely, Margaret. Like a princess.

MARGARET: What do you think, Cinderella?

CINDERELLA: *(Standing.)* Oh, you are both very beautiful and elegant. The prince will have a very difficult time choosing between you.

STEPMOTHER: And, Cinderella, have you completed all your chores?

CINDERELLA: Yes, Stepmother. I did all my daily chores, and I washed the drapes and the windows...and the linens... and I swept every floor.

STEPMOTHER: Well that's wonderful, dear; you'll be coming with us then.

(CINDERELLA perks up, almost smiles.)

Scene 6 - 25

ELINORA: Mother, no!

MARGARET: She can't!

STEPMOTHER: Now, girls, we had an agreement. Cinderella deserves to come along. Well what are you waiting for child? You need to wash, get in your dress. We must leave immediately.

CINDERELLA: I don't have a dress. I didn't have time.

STEPMOTHER: Oh, my dear girl, that's a shame. But don't fret about it. There will be other royal events to attend. Perhaps next time.

CINDERELLA: Yes, Stepmother.

STEPMOTHER: Come, girls, it's time to go.

(MARGARET and ELINORA scream with delight and exit via the kitchen door with STEPMOTHER following.)

STEPMOTHER: *(Spitefully, just before exiting.)* And besides, you didn't say that you killed the mouse.

CINDERELLA: *(Sitting at the kitchen table.)* Oh well, she's right. I'm sure there will be other royal events. There will be another time for me, I suppose.

CLARA: *(Appearing from the magic entrance gap at the fireplace wall.)* Oh no, dear, tonight is your time. By tomorrow it will be too late.

CINDERELLA: *(Startled to her feet.)* Who are you? Where did you come from?

CLARA: Who do you think I am, Cinderella?

CINDERELLA: How do you know my name?

CLARA: I know everything about you.

CINDERELLA: You do?

CLARA: I've been watching you for quite some time now.

CINDERELLA: You have?

CLARA: Why yes, dear, I'm your Fairy Godmother.

CINDERELLA: Oh, well...I'm sorry *Godmother*, but I don't believe in *fairies*.

CLARA: So you explain how I popped into the room, and how I know who you are.

CINDERELLA: Perhaps you're a witch.

CLARA: *(Insulted.)* Well I never!

CINDERELLA: Or maybe an angel...maybe you're my guardian angel.
CLARA: What does it really matter, dear? Angel...Fairy Godmother...the point is, I'm here to help you.
CINDERELLA: To help me? To help me with what?
CLARA: *(Waving her wand in circles in the air.)* To get to the ball, Cinderella.
CINDERELLA: *(Shocked by the wand.)* Madam, I will have nothing to do with witchcraft or magic.
CLARA: Please, don't worry, dear. I assure you I am here with the approval of the- *(Looking and pointing up.)* -highest authority.
CINDERELLA: You <u>are</u> an angel!
CLARA: Let's not quibble over titles. We have a lot of work to do, and you are late already! *(Crossing to the kitchen door and looking out the window.)* Let's see. You will need transportation. The big pumpkin at the edge of the patch should do nicely.

(CLARA starts waving her wand in circles.)

SFX: Magic "glimmer" starts

CINDERELLA: A pumpkin?

(CLARA closes her eyes and flips her wrist.)

SFX: Gunshot.

CLARA: *(Shocked at her success.)* Oh! Isn't it lovely!
CINDERELLA: Oh my goodness! I think it's a carriage!
CLARA: Of course it is, dear.
CINDERELLA: *(With a puzzled look.)* But won't it need wheels?
CLARA: *(Looking again then walking away from the window.)* Oh...yes, I suppose. Don't worry I'll get to that.

(THEODORE THE MOUSE comes out of his mouse hole and onto the fireplace mantle.)

CINDERELLA: And horses.
CLARA: Yes dear, details, details. I'll get to those too.

CINDERELLA: And a coachman, unless you want me to drive myself to the ball.

CLARA: *(Spotting THEODORE THE MOUSE, she points the wand in his direction and starts waving it in circles.)* A coachman...you're little friend should do nicely.

SFX: Magic "glimmer" starts

CINDERELLA: Theodore!

(THEODORE THE MOUSE runs across the mantle just as CLARA flips her wrist.)

SFX: Gunshot.

(THEODORE the coachman enters from the magic gap at the fireplace. A pair of white gloves hangs from his belt. He walks formally with both hands behind his back.)

CINDERELLA: Theodore? Is that you?

THEODORE: *(Bowing to her.)* Yes, it is I, my lady.

(THEODORE brings one hand forward as he bows. The hand is covered with mouse hair and the fingernails are black. Everyone is shocked. He checks his other hand and finds it to be normal.)

CLARA: I didn't get that quite right, did I?

THEODORE: I would think not.

CLARA: *(Pointing the wand back at THEODORE.)* I'll just give that another try.

(CINDERELLA crosses between CLARA and THEODORE to block her shot.)

THEODORE AND CINDERELLA: No!

CINDERELLA: Look, Theodore, you have gloves. Perhaps you should wear them.

CLARA: Oh well, we need to keep moving. Are you ready, Cinderella?

CINDERELLA: Ready?

CLARA: *(Pointing the wand at CINDERELLA.)* You're next.

CINDERELLA: Oh, please don't point that at me.

CLARA: But, Cinderella dear, you need a dress.

(See the Production Kit for magic trick details that may accompany the remaining dialog in this scene. Or, if magic is not desired, see the Scene 6 Alternate Ending at the end of this script. The alternate ending picks up at this point.)

(CINDERELLA, picks up the laundry basket, places it on the table and removes a stack of folded linens from the top.)

THEODORE: Don't let her do it, Cinderella, it's too dangerous. She might do something you can't cover with a glove!

CINDERELLA: *(Pulling a dull dress from the laundry basket.)* Well, here. Can you make this into a pretty dress?

CLARA: Let me see. It is a bit dull, isn't it?

CINDERELLA: *(Dropping the bodice back into the basket.)* Well, yes, but...

CLARA: *(Picking up the hem and exposing the inside of the dress.)* Some very nice stitching, dear.

CINDERELLA: Oh, thank you.

CLARA: *(Placing the hem down with only the inside of the dress facing up.)* And the lining is in wonderful condition. Does it fit you properly, dear?

CINDERELLA: Yes.

CLARA: Then the size should be right.

CINDERELLA: I think so, yes.

CLARA: Let's give it a shot, shall we?

CINDERELLA: Okay.

(CLARA points the wand at the dress. Seeing the wand again pointed in her direction, CINDERELLA steps away. CLARA starts spinning her wand.)

SFX: Magic "glimmer" starts

(Clara flips the wand with a snap.)

SFX: Gunshot.

CLARA: *(Pulling the lower part of the dress out to hang over the edge of the basket and revealing elegant fabric.)* Isn't that lovely material?!

CINDERELLA: *(Picking up a bodice of the same material that has a large burnt hole at the shoulder and a missing sleeve.)* It's not exactly what I had in mind.

CLARA: Oh my goodness! I suppose it is a good thing you weren't wearing that. I think I can fix it.

CINDERELLA: Maybe it's just not meant to be.

CLARA: *(Pulls a large piece of the material from the dress. Confused)* Well, there's even a bit of extra material.

CINDERELLA: *(Dropping the bodice.)* It's just a mess, and there isn't time.

CLARA: *(Covering the basket with the extra material.)* Oh, we mustn't dwell on the negative, dear. There's always hope. I just need a little more practice with this silly little wand.

CINDERELLA: Practice?

CLARA: No worries, Cinderella. Let's just try again, shall we?

CINDERELLA: Yes, please.

(CLARA starts spinning the wand again, but longer, more concentrated and more serious than before.)

SFX: Magic "glimmer" starts

(CLARA flips the wand in a more graceful gesture.)

SFX: Gunshot.

(CINDERELLA steps up, takes the extra material off, drops it on the stack of linens and slowly pulls out a beautiful dress made of the same material as the previously damaged prop.)

CINDERELLA: Oh my goodness! It's the most beautiful dress I've ever seen!

CLARA: It is, isn't it?

THEODORE: Spectacular!

CINDERELLA: *(Hugging CLARA.)* Oh, thank you, Fairy Godmother! Thank you so much!

CLARA: You're welcome, dear.

CINDERELLA: *(Crossing to the hallway exit.)* I must try it on. *(Pause.)* Theodore, we're going to the ball!

THEODORE: That's right! I am going to a grand ball at the royal palace!

CLARA: Yes, you are.

CINDERELLA: *(To CLARA)* Thank you, I don't know how I could ever repay you.

CLARA: Just have a good time, dear. Oh and I almost forgot; there's a deadline.

CINDERELLA: A deadline?

THEODORE: But what about her shoes?

CLARA: At the stroke of midnight, everything will go back to the way it was before.

CINDERELLA: Yes, what about my shoes? I can't go in these.

CLARA: Leave them to me, dear. Now go get changed. There's no time to waste.

(CINDERELLA steps out of her shoes and quickly exits via the hallway. THEODORE picks up the shoes.)

CLARA: *(Picking up the extra piece of material.)* Let me see now. We want them to complement the dress.

THEODORE: Most certainly, madam.

CLARA: *(Dancing with the material like a dress)* A Grand Ball...dancing and romance-

THEODORE: Not without shoes.

CLARA: Oh, yes, of course.

(THEODORE tries to hand the shoes to CLARA but instead she leaves them in his hand and places the material over them.)

THEODORE: Madam, you don't expect to do that while I'm holding them?!

CLARA: Oh, well it is perfectly safe.

THEODORE: No, no, no, I don't think-

CLARA: Come now, Theodore, are you a man or a mou... Oh, that's right. Don't worry, Theodore, dear. Just hold still.

(CLARA begins spinning her wand again.)

Scene 6 - 31

SFX: Magic "glimmer" starts

(THEODORE gets a scared look, winces and squeaks like a mouse.)

SFX: Gunshot.

CLARA: *(Pulling the material off of the shoes, taking them from THEODORE and placing them on the table.)* I believe I've outdone myself this time. Glass slippers.
THEODORE: *(Checking his hand to make sure he still has all of his fingers.)* Oh, yes. Thank you, thank you, thank you.
CLARA: *(Crossing to the kitchen door.)* They're absolutely stunning. But there is still so much to do. Come with me, Theodore. We still need horses and a carriage with wheels.
JAMES: *(Appearing from the gap at the fireplace wall.)* Clara?
CLARA: Oh! Mr. Ashton, how nice of you to drop in.

(THEODORE gets a puzzled look on his face.)

JAMES: Thank you, Clara. You really made a difference this time. It means a lot to me.
CLARA: Oh it was certainly my pleasure, Mr. Ashton. It means a lot to all of us.

(CLARA exits and THEODORE follows.)

SLOW FADE TO BLACK

SCENE 7

Mission Accomplished

Mr. Richardson's Office, the same evening.

SETTING: The Department of Minor Miracles and Blessings

AT RISE: MR RICHARDSON sits behind his desk and is writing on a form with a gold pen.

SFX: Telephone Ringing

MR RICHARDSON: *(Picks up desk phone receiver.)* Department of Minor Miracles and Blessings, this is Mr. Richardson.
CLARA (O.S.): Hello, Mr. Richardson. This is Clara!
MR RICHARDSON: Clara? I hope-
CLARA (O.S.): Wasn't it wonderful, sir? Oh, you were watching, weren't you?
MR RICHARDSON: Yes, Clara, and I was just completing your Miracle Execution Form, but-
CLARA (O.S.): Did you see how beautiful she looked in her dress?
MR RICHARDSON: Yes, I must admit-
CLARA (O.S.): And the carriage! It has to be the most elegant carriage I have ever seen!
MR RICHARDSON: Yes, Clara, you did a wonderful job with the carriage.
CLARA (O.S.): I am just amazed at how well mice work as horses...and Theodore turned out to be a very clever coachman.
MR RICHARDSON: Yes, he certainly-
CLARA (O.S.): Oh, Mr. Richardson, you probably couldn't see her shoes from up there, but they are the most beautiful glass slippers!
MR RICHARDSON: Really?
CLARA (O.S.): Elegant, graceful, pure — she absolutely glows in them.
MR RICHARDSON: Excellent, Clara. You did a very nice job.
CLARA (O.S.): Thank you, sir.

MR RICHARDSON: Did Cinderella understand the deadline she has?

CLARA (O.S.): Oh yes...well...I know I told her. Let me think. The stroke of midnight...

MR RICHARDSON: Clara, it is important that she understands.

CLARA (O.S.): I believe she said...that's funny, I don't really recall-

MR RICHARDSON: You did tell her, didn't you?

CLARA (O.S.): Of course I told her. But it was all so exciting. I can't seem to remember what she thought of it.

MR RICHARDSON: It doesn't matter if she liked it or not. It all ends at midnight. Those are the rules.

CLARA (O.S.): Yes, Mr. Richardson, I told her the rules.

MR RICHARDSON: Good. Now, Clara, about this telephone call.

CLARA (O.S.): Is there something wrong?

MR RICHARDSON: You could have given me a full report when you returned.

CLARA (O.S.): But it was so exciting-

MR RICHARDSON: It is a long distance call, Clara.

CLARA (O.S.): Yes...quite.

MR RICHARDSON: Did you put the call on the company card?

CLARA (O.S.): It is the most convenient.

MR RICHARDSON: Yes. Well...

CLARA (O.S.): Am I in any trouble?

MR RICHARDSON: *(Pause. Somewhat reluctantly.)* Bring your travel expense report to me before you turn it in to your supervisor...I'll authorize the call under my department's budget.

CLARA (O.S.): Oh, thank you, Mr. Richardson. That's very kind of you.

MR RICHARDSON: Why don't you stop by my office when you get in and we'll take a moment to check on Cinderella.

CLARA (O.S.): That would be wonderful. I'll see you soon.

MR RICHARDSON: Have a nice flight.

(He hangs up the receiver and goes back to writing.)

SLOW FADE TO BLACK

[Start of optional mini scene to be played in front of the curtain during the scene change.]

> *(GUINEVERE enters followed by CASSANDRA and the other MAIDENs attending the ball. All enter at one edge of the stage and cross "gracefully" to the other edge where the CAPTAIN and ROYAL PAGE are waiting. Some ladies may have a gentleman escort. STEPMOTHER, MARGARET and ELINORA enter last.)*

CAPTAIN: Ladies, please form an orderly line.

MARGARET: Mother, we are late! I wanted to be the first in line.

A MAIDEN: Yes, the early bird gets the worm, as they say.

MARGARET: We are at the end of the line!

A MAIDEN: *(Looking back offstage)* Oh please, we are all at the front of the line. There are many more carriages still arriving.

MARGARET: Mother!

STEPMOTHER: I'm working on it, dear.

CAPTAIN: You will each be introduced to his royal highness, Prince Henry the Third, in due order.

> *(The CAPTAIN exits)*

A MAIDEN: Oh my goodness, I'm so nervous. I'm going to meet the prince! What do you say to a prince? Oh, is my hair okay? How do I look?

STEPMOTHER: Let me see, dear child. *(Pushing forward in line she then spins the MAIDEN around while moving her backward in line. Other MAIDENs ad lib "Who does she think she is?", "Excuse you", type lines)* Oh don't worry your pretty little head. You really don't have a chance anyway.

A MAIDEN: I can't believe she just said that!

STEPMOTHER: *(Touching the grand drape)* My heavens, the palace draperies are exquisite. The softest thing I've ever touched.

(All MAIDENs and ELINORA turn upstage and start touching the drapes and ad lib lines about "beautiful", "soft" or "not that soft", etc. STEPMOTHER and MARGARET rush to the front of the line but are stopped at CASSANDRA.)

CASSANDRA: I don't think so.
ROYAL PAGE: Ladies! Please do not touch the draperies!

(MAIDENs and ELINORA step back into their places.)

STEPMOTHER: *(To ROYAL PAGE)* Do forgive them. They are all just foolish children. It comes from bad upbringing.

(MAIDENs ad lib lines in shock and disgust: "I'll rip her hair out", "No, what if I ruin my dress", etc.)

ELINORA: *(Still stuck at the back of the line)* Mother?!
STEPMOTHER: Elinora! How did you wander so far away from your loving mother? Come up here, my sweet child.

(MAIDENs ad lib more angry lines as ELINORA timidly passes them.)

MARGARET: Mother, I'm still not first.
STEPMOTHER: Patience, Margaret dear.
CASSANDRA: Patience? Huh! You'll need enough patience to stay third in line.
STEPMOTHER: You impertinent little girl. You will watch your tongue-
CASSANDRA: I'm on to your tricks and games, old woman-
STEPMOTHER: *(Yelling)* Old woman?!
ROYAL PAGE: Ladies, please maintain composure and appropriate decorum within the royal palace.

(Attitudes return to their original fake "gracefulness")

CASSANDRA: *(Through a faked sweet smile)* And you won't be tricking me just to satisfy your spoiled brat.
MARGARET: Mother!

STEPMOTHER: Not to worry, dear. When you become the new princess, hers will be the first head to roll.

SLOW FADE TO BLACK

[End of optional mini scene section]

SCENE 8

Blind Ambition

The Royal Palace Ballroom, 8:00 p.m.

SETTING: The Royal Palace Ballroom

AT RISE: The time on a grand-royal clock is 8:00. The KING and QUEEN are seated on their respective thrones. The PRINCE, NICHOLAS and the CAPTAIN are also in the scene.

PRINCE: *(To the KING.)* You are being completely unreasonable!
KING: You will watch your tone with me, young man.
PRINCE: *(Sarcastically)* A grand ball giving every starry-eyed girl in the kingdom an invitation to come use her...feminine... persuasions...to catch me like a carnival prize!
QUEEN: He has a point, dear.
KING: He is not cooperating.
QUEEN: *(To the PRINCE.)* Really, sweetheart, your father and I have been very patient in the matter. Your future is important to us.
PRINCE: But, Mother, a royal decree forcing me to find a bride and marry within fifteen days? It's absurd!
KING: I'm not getting any younger, and you obviously need a bit of a push.
PRINCE: I am the laughing stock of the entire kingdom!
QUEEN: Certainly not, sweetheart.
PRINCE: The rumors are flying everywhere, Mother! They're even talking about Father threatening to throw me in the dungeon if I don't cooperate.
KING: Maybe we'll just skip right to a beheading.
PRINCE: *(In disgust.)* Hu!
QUEEN: Henry, stop teasing the boy.
PRINCE: I am not a boy, Mother.
KING: No, you are a young man, a prince with royal obligations.
PRINCE: Obligations, Father? To give you grandchildren?

KING: *(Trying to cover.)* You must...continue the royal bloodline.

PRINCE: The royal bloodline? You just want a little boy to play catch with, or a little girl to sit on your lap. It has nothing to do with bloodline.

QUEEN: Oh, sweetheart, no...not just one or two...we expect lots of grandchildren.

KING: Six is a good number.

QUEEN: At least three boys and three girls if you don't mind.

PRINCE: Unbelievable.

KING: Henry, you may not like it and you may be embarrassed by the whole thing, but this ball is for your own good. There are many beautiful young ladies in my kingdom, most of whom you have never met.

QUEEN: Just look at this as an opportunity to expand your horizons.

PRINCE: And what about love, mother? Do you really want me to just pick the prettiest girl I see, and that's it?

QUEEN: No, sweetheart, your father and I want you to be happy. But you must meet a girl before you can fall in love.

PRINCE: But Mother-

QUEEN: You just need to find a girl who has the strength and ability to be a leader — a queen in the making.

KING: And there's nothing wrong with falling in love with a pretty girl while you're at it.

PRINCE: That is just the trouble, Father. If I am to fall in love, it must be with the girl's heart. But every girl coming here tonight will be hiding her true heart behind her beauty and flirtations. And, I am a man. How do I stop my eyes from clouding my vision?

QUEEN: *(Pause. To the KING.)* Oh, Henry...he's right. Perhaps this is a bad idea.

KING: Don't be ridiculous. He has simply gone mad. *(To the PRINCE.)* Of course they will all be in their best dresses, as elegant as they can be. And it is my hope that many of them will be breathtakingly beautiful. It's part of the package, my boy. Learn to appreciate it.

QUEEN: Henry! If I didn't know better I would think this ball was more for your benefit than his.

KING: It is for me! I want grandchildren! And pretty grandchildren would be best.
PRINCE: Really, Father, you are exasperating.
KING: If you are so worried about- *(Mocking him.)* -your eyes clouding your vision, then why don't you wear a blindfold.
PRINCE: A blindfold.
QUEEN: Sweetheart, your father just-
PRINCE: *(Looks around. Crosses to the CAPTAIN and removes a sash from his uniform.)* An excellent idea, Father. A blindfold.
QUEEN: Sweetheart, you can't be serious.
PRINCE: *(Tying the sash over his eyes.)* Completely so, Mother.
QUEEN: I insist you take that wretched thing off this instant!
PRINCE: No, Mother. My heart must choose my princess. I will not allow my eyes to decide for me.
QUEEN: *(To the KING.)* Henry, what have you done?
KING: I spoke in jest. He has obviously gone mad.
PRINCE: *(Walking blindly forward and nearly falling)* I am not a madman, Father.
KING: And how will you get about without falling on your face?
PRINCE: Nicholas!
NICHOLAS: Yes, Your Highness.
PRINCE: My attendant will be my eyes this evening. Won't you, Nicholas?
NICHOLAS: As you wish, Your Highness.
QUEEN: *(To the PRINCE.)* Be reasonable, sweetheart. You are expected to dance with the young ladies. If you lead with a blindfold it will be disastrous.
PRINCE: *(Ponders for a moment.)* I will let them lead, Mother. What better way to find a girl 'who has the strength and ability to be a leader — a queen in the making?'
QUEEN: *(To the KING.)* This is all your fault! You and your royal big mouth.
KING: He gets it from your side of the family.
PRINCE: Nicholas, I trust you to make certain I dance, or spend some measure of time, with every lady attending the ball this evening. Do you understand?

NICHOLAS: I understand. But as your friend, Henry, I must tell you...I think you should reconsider. There will be a lot to look at this evening.

PRINCE: Just try to keep me from running into anything.

NICHOLAS: An unusual challenge, Sire.

PRINCE: *(Referring to the blindfold.)* Make sure the knot is tight. If any try to unmask me, it should not come off easily.

NICHOLAS: Yes, your majesty.

SFX: A Brass Fanfare announces the start of the ball and is followed by waltz music through the remainder of the scene.

ROYAL PAGE: *(Entering before each announcement and exiting immediately after.)* The lady Guinevere Needham.

(GUINEVERE enters and curtsies to the KING, QUEEN and PRINCE. She is visibly puzzled by the blindfold.)

ROYAL PAGE: The lady Cassandra Wakefield.

(CASSANDRA enters, similar to the previous.)

ROYAL PAGE: The matron Evelyn Ashton, widow of James Ashton and her daughters; the ladies Margaret and Elinora.

(STEPMOTHER, MARGARET and ELINORA enter and curtsy. MARGARET and ELINORA are visibly upset with each other, exchanging spiteful gazes.)

(Additional ladies {and gentlemen escorts, if desired} may be introduced at the ball. However, the ROYAL PAGE announces them in mime as the dialog continues.)

NICHOLAS: *(Leading GUINEVERE to the PRINCE.)* My lady, Guinevere, I present his royal highness, Prince Henry the Third.

GUINEVERE: *(Curtsies.)* Your majesty.

PRINCE: *(With a slight bow but in the wrong direction)* Lady Guinevere, might I have the honor of a dance?

(NICHOLAS corrects the PRINCE's postion.)

GUINEVERE: *(Awkwardly, because of the blindfold.)* Well... yes...your highness.

(They begin to dance in a stiff tug-of-war style. NICHOLAS realizes he will need another lady immediately and crosses to CASSANDRA. However, MARGARET pushes her way forward almost knocking CASSANDRA to the floor. NICHOLAS gestures for MARGARET to step forward and then cuts into the PRINCE's dance.)

(The KING dances with each lady immediately after the PRINCE.)

NICHOLAS: Your highness...the lady Margaret.
PRINCE: My lady.
MARGARET: May I ask, Your Highness, are we playing a party game?
PRINCE: I beg your pardon?
MARGARET: The blindfold; it looks simply ridiculous.
PRINCE: I see. Well, yes. You've heard of "Pin the Tail on the Donkey?"
MARGARET: Certainly.
PRINCE: This is called "Pin the Donkey on the Prince."
MARGARET: Oh, I would like to play.
PRINCE: Shall we dance?

(MARGARET and the PRINCE dance "aggressively". MARGARET runs the PRINCE into other dancers and NICHOLAS breaks in. ELINORA takes this as her opportunity and approaches the PRINCE without an introduction.)

ELINORA: Prince Henry, I knew the moment I entered the room and our eyes met that it was true love.
PRINCE: Our eyes met, my lady?
ELINORA: I mean...our...err...I...I saw you, and I knew in my heart-
PRINCE: Really? In your heart, my lady?
ELINORA: *(Fanning herself, she begins to sway dizzily.)* My goodness it is so warm in here. I think I might need to...sit...down.

(She faints but NICHOLAS runs in to catch her.)

NICHOLAS: I've got you!

PRINCE: Nicholas, what's happening?

NICHOLAS: You seem to be slaying them in the aisles, Your Highness.

PRINCE: *(Sarcastically)* Wonderful.

NICHOLAS: She'll be sitting this one out.

PRINCE: Very well. Bring me another.

NICHOLAS: In just a moment, Your Highness.

> *(The volume level of the dance music rises. ELINORA revives and wobbles back to her family. CASSANDRA sees her opportunity and introduces herself to the PRINCE in mime. They begin dancing together. If desired, other ladies attending the ball may now cut in on each other and dance with the PRINCE in various comical styles.)*
>
> *SLOW FADE TO BLACK*

SCENE 9

A Breath of Fresh Air

At the Royal Garden Footbridge, nearly 10:00 p.m.

SETTING:　　The Royal Garden Footbridge

AT RISE:　　NICHOLAS is leading the PRINCE to one side of a narrow footbridge in the royal gardens.

PRINCE: I just need a bit of a break.

NICHOLAS: All right, I think it's safe now.

PRINCE: *(Reaching behind his head to work on the blindfold's knot.)* Do you think anyone would miss me if I just hid myself in the garden for the rest of the evening?

NICHOLAS: You must be joking. Henry, every eye has been on you for the entire evening. And right now? Their dresses are pressed against the windows as they wait for you to appear again.

PRINCE: *(Hands springing away from the blindfold.)* You don't think they could slip past the guardsmen and hunt me down?

NICHOLAS: It is a distinct possibility.

PRINCE: They are a pack of hungry cats fighting for the chance to pounce on a blind mouse.

NICHOLAS: I find it interesting how unreservedly they stare at a man when they know he cannot catch them doing so. It is quite amusing to watch.

PRINCE: Nicholas, it's good to know you have been entertained at my expense.

NICHOLAS: By your design.

PRINCE: No, it is my father's design.

NICHOLAS: The king is certainly enjoying himself this evening. Just like you, he has danced with every lady. I believe he is more interested in finding a daughter-in-law than you are in finding a bride.

PRINCE: I am exhausted. What do I do now, Nicholas?

NICHOLAS: You gave your heart a chance, Henry. Have you fallen madly in love?

PRINCE: No.

NICHOLAS: Then maybe it's time to give your eyes a chance.

PRINCE: I don't know.

NICHOLAS: Just last month, Henry, we were on a hunt and I was complaining about the narrow trail you chose to take down that mountainside. Do you remember?

PRINCE: Yes, you coward.

NICHOLAS: You told me that riding a horse down a mountainside can be uncomfortable and perilous...but you can still enjoy the view.

PRINCE: What's your point?

NICHOLAS: Then you said that brave riders select even more difficult paths simply to get a better view.

PRINCE: Are you calling me a coward?

NICHOLAS: Henry, if you don't make a choice tonight your father will certainly have a selection for you. You're going down that mountainside whether you like it or not and there is no way to tell what dangers lie ahead. I think you should make sure to choose a path that has a nice view.

PRINCE: *(He pauses and then starts trying to unknot his blindfold again.)* You're right. The game is over.

(The PRINCE struggles to untie the knot. CINDERELLA enters from a house aisle on the opposite side of the footbridge.)

NICHOLAS: What is she doing out here?

PRINCE: *(Stops working at the knot.)* What's that?

NICHOLAS: There is a young lady wandering in the garden. She doesn't look familiar. I think she may be arriving late.

PRINCE: Why would she enter through the garden? It's such a maze; she could easily get lost.

NICHOLAS: She's coming this way. *(Stunned by her beauty.)* I really think you should take that blindfold off.

(NICHOLAS crosses the footbridge and approaches CINDERELLA. They talk in whispers.)

PRINCE: It stays on until after we dance. It doesn't matter if she is the ugliest girl of the lot or the prettiest; I just need to finish this charade as I started it. Introduce us. *(Pause)* Nicholas?...Nicholas?

(CINDERELLA resists a little but NICHOLAS leads her to the PRINCE.)

NICHOLAS: The lady refuses to give me her name. She says an introduction to royalty is not necessary; she only wants a chance to see the palace and — in her own words — 'dance at a grand ball with anyone but the prince.'
PRINCE: Really? Where is she?

(NICHOLAS leads CINDERELLA up the footbridge and then places her hand in the PRINCE's. The PRINCE turns his head sharply. NICHOLAS exits quietly the way he came.)

PRINCE: My lady...do I know you? I feel as though we have met before.
CINDERELLA: Why would you say that? You can't see me, and only now have heard my voice.
PRINCE: Yes, you are correct. I suppose I'm being a bit ridiculous.
CINDERELLA: No, Your Highness, not ridiculous at all.
PRINCE: Then I do know you?
CINDERELLA: I'm afraid we have never met.
PRINCE: I have never stomped on your toe while dancing?
CINDERELLA: *(Amused.)* Certainly not.
PRINCE: Then why do you refuse to dance with me this evening?
CINDERELLA: Please forgive me, Your Highness. I mean no offense. I just don't want to be part of your father's...of the king's decree. It's not right that you should be forced into this.
PRINCE: So you prefer I be thrown into the dungeon?
CINDERELLA: Oh no, Your Highness!
PRINCE: If I choose, of my own free will, to ask you to dance with me?
CINDERELLA: Oh, no...I don't want anyone to...I mean...
PRINCE: If I ask you, not as a prince, but as a gentleman asking from his heart to have the honor of a lady's company?
CINDERELLA: I feel a bit like a mouse backed into a corner.
PRINCE: *(He laughs playfully.)* I know exactly what you mean.
CINDERELLA: Very well, I will dance with you, Prince Henry.

PRINCE: My lady, you know my name but I still do not know yours. Perhaps you are hiding it because it is the name of a wanted criminal.

CINDERELLA: And perhaps you have the shifty eyes of a thief.

PRINCE: Point taken, my lady. You win that round. But don't you want to know why I wear this blindfold?

CINDERELLA: With a palace full of beautiful ladies and your father's unreasonable deadline, the answer is obvious.

PRINCE: Excellent deduction.

CINDERELLA: It is very noble. But you are a bit silly looking.

(They both laugh.)

PRINCE: Nicholas? Nicholas? Where is my attendant? He is supposed to lead me about.

CINDERELLA: I believe he left us, Your Majesty, but I can lead you back.

(They start to exit together.)

PRINCE: Tell me. Why did you come through the garden rather than being properly received at the palace gate?

CINDERELLA: I asked my coachman to stop because it was so breathtaking... like looking into the Garden of Eden. When I realized I could get to the palace on foot, I sent my carriage without me.

PRINCE: *(As they exit.)* And you say I am the silly one.

SLOW FADE TO BLACK

SCENE 10

Belle of the Ball

The Royal Palace Ballroom, after 11:00 p.m.

SETTING: The Royal Palace Ballroom

AT RISE: The time on the palace clock is now 11:23. Romantic dance music underscores the scene at a low level. The PRINCE and CINDERELLA dance together throughout the scene. They mime conversation with each other, smile and laugh frequently. The rest of the room is divided into three groups of conversion; 1) KING, QUEEN and NICHOLAS, 2) STEPMOTHER, MARGARET and ELINORA, and 3) THEODORE, GUINEVERE, CASSANDRA and other MAIDENS as desired. The CAPTAIN stands at attention between the thrones and the clock. The general lighting is romantically dim. Specialty/follow lighting spots conversations as they occur.

ELINORA: Is he going to dance with that girl all night? I still haven't had my turn.

MARGARET: You had your chance. You were a disaster.

ELINORA: Mother, Margaret is insulting me again.

STEPMOTHER: *(Watching CINDERELLA.)* That girl. She seems a bit familiar.

ELINORA: Mother! What about me!

STEPMOTHER: Don't worry girls, I'm certain you both made an impression on Prince Henry. He's just obligated to dance with everyone.

MARGARET: But he's been dancing with her for well over an hour.

ELINORA: And he still hasn't danced with me.

STEPMOTHER: *(Again distracted by CINDERELLA.)* Yes, it is strange. And I just can't place where I've seen that girl before.

(The lighting shifts.)

QUEEN: Goodness, their endurance reminds me of when we were young, Henry.

KING: I still have it, my dear. I danced with every lady this evening.

QUEEN: You mean every beautiful...young...lady. You didn't even dance with me, Henry!

KING: Oh darling, I didn't realize.

QUEEN: Honestly, I don't know where your son learned to be so noble, with you as an example.

KING: You cut me to the quick.

QUEEN: I know you're anxious to meet your new daughter-in-law, even before your son does.

KING: I'm afraid he may have beaten me to it.

QUEEN: She certainly has kept his interest for quite some time.

KING: Yes, she is the only one with whom I have not had the opportunity to dance.

QUEEN: And by my estimation, the prettiest here.

KING: Now you are just trying to torment me. *(Pause. Getting visibly impatient.)* Oh...I'm just going to cut in!

QUEEN: Henry!

NICHOLAS: *(Stepping in front of the KING as he tries to cross toward the PRINCE.)* Your Majesty!

KING: Yes, Nicholas?

NICHOLAS: If I could sir...may I...I...uh...

KING: Speak up man!

NICHOLAS: Might I enquire what you are doing, Sire?

KING: Not that it is any of your business, but I am about to introduce myself to the young lady dancing with my son.

(The KING steps around NICHOLAS but NICHOLAS circles and stops him again.)

KING: What are you doing?

NICHOLAS: With my apologies, Your Majesty. Your son commanded me to keep everyone away while he danced with the young lady.

KING: Well he wasn't talking about me.

NICHOLAS: He mentioned you specifically, Sire.

KING: Well...I.... Really?
NICHOLAS: Yes, Your Majesty.

(The KING returns to his throne followed by NICHOLAS.)

(The lighting shifts.)

(The following dialog may be split between two or more MAIDENs including GUINEVERE and CASSANDRA.)

A MAIDEN: Who is she?
A MAIDEN: No one seems to know.
A MAIDEN: Every lady in the entire kingdom is here. Someone must know who she is.
A MAIDEN: What I would like to know is how he managed to pick the most beautiful girl while wearing a blindfold.
A MAIDEN: *(A bit spiteful.)* She is pretty, isn't she?
A MAIDEN: Please, tell me, where do you get a dress like that?
A MAIDEN: And those shoes!
A MAIDEN: I know!
A MAIDEN: I suppose it is time we just admit defeat.
A MAIDEN: Yes. It was exciting, but I think it's time to go home.
A MAIDEN: If she just didn't look so sweet...
A MAIDEN: ...it would be easy to hate her.
A MAIDEN: But she's just so elegant...
A MAIDEN: And graceful...
A MAIDEN: And incredibly kind and gentle and loving and generous-
A MAIDEN: Do you know her?!
THEODORE: We're very close.
A MAIDEN: What's her name?!
A MAIDEN: You must tell us!
THEODORE: Cinde- *(Realizes he might be making a mistake. Pointing to CINDERELLA.)* Did you mean that girl? I don't know who she is. I thought you were talking about someone else.
A MAIDEN: You're hiding something.
THEODORE: *(To GUINEVERE.)* Have you tried the cheesy hors d'oeuvres? They're delicious.

(The lighting shifts.)

QUEEN: Do you think she likes children?
KING: I get the feeling she will make a wonderful mother. They will certainly be handsome children, don't you think?
QUEEN: Oh, yes, quite handsome at that.
KING: *(Reaching to hold his wife's hand.)* Even if only two or three grandchildren–
QUEEN: I'm sorry, Henry, I don't know why we didn't have more of our own.
KING: It just wasn't meant to be, my dear.

(The lighting shifts.)

(JAMES appears from the gap between the clock and stone wall. He crosses in front of STEPMOTHER and looks at CINDERELLA.)

JAMES: Ella, you look magnificent, a beautiful young woman. You look more like your mother every day. I am so proud of you.
STEPMOTHER: *(A rare "soft" moment. She looks "through" JAMES to see the couple dancing.)* There's something about the prince. Something very special.
MARGARET: Yes, mother. Obviously.
STEPMOTHER: Something about him...he reminds me of James.
JAMES: I thought you had completely forgotten, Evelyn.
ELINORA: Who is James?
MARGARET: Really, Elinora, you are so dim.
ELINORA: Mother!
STEPMOTHER: Margaret, she wouldn't remember him. She was very young.
MARGARET: I suppose. But she's heard the name.
STEPMOTHER: Not often.
JAMES: No. Not often enough.
STEPMOTHER: James was your stepfather, dear.
MARGARET: Did you love him, Mother?
JAMES: Evelyn, there was something between us, wasn't there?
STEPMOTHER: I don't really remember. I do know that he loved me, more than your father did.

JAMES: You loved me, Evelyn. You just don't want to remember, do you?
ELINORA: Oh, you mean Cinderella's father, don't you?
STEPMOTHER: *(Glancing back at CINDERELLA on the dance floor.)* Yes, dear. Cinderella's father... *(Making the connection.)* Cinderella...it's Cinderella!
ELINORA: What?!
MARGARET: It can't be!
STEPMOTHER: *(Angrily.)* What is she doing here?!
JAMES: Evelyn, no! Your anger is not with her!
MARGARET: Mother, what are you going to do?
STEPMOTHER: *(She starts to approach CINDERELLA.)* I am going to put her in her place!
JAMES: I hope you can forgive me for this!

(JAMES bends over and ruffles STEPMOTHERS dress into the air. STEPMOTHER screams and pushes her dress down. General lighting becomes brighter and the music stops as everyone looks at STEPMOTHER in shock.)

ELINORA: Mother, what's wrong?!
MARGARET: You're embarrassing us.
PRINCE: What on earth is going on?

(The CAPTAIN and NICHOLAS cross to STEPMOTHER.)

CINDERELLA: Just a bit of trouble from an upset guest I think.
PRINCE: Shall we continue then?
CINDERELLA: Could we rest for a bit and get some fresh air?
PRINCE: As you wish, my lady with no name.
CINDERELLA: *(She laughs and leads the PRINCE as they exit.)* Stop calling me that.
STEPMOTHER: She is an impostor, a fraud.
NICHOLAS: What are you talking about, madam?
STEPMOTHER: I must speak to the prince about that girl!
JAMES: Don't do this, Evelyn!
NICHOLAS: I have instructions to keep everyone away from the prince.
CAPTAIN: What allegation do you have against the young lady, madam?

NICHOLAS: Is she not an eligible maiden? Do you know the girl?

STEPMOTHER: Do I know her? Well I... No, I don't know who she is.

JAMES: *(Sympathetically)* You feel guilty about the way you treat her, don't you?

STEPMOTHER: But my daughter Elinora has not danced with the prince. That conniving gold-digger has completely monopolized his time.

NICHOLAS: Your daughter met and spoke with Prince Henry. There was never a promise of anything more.

STEPMOTHER: But she must dance with the prince. He is being unfair.

NICHOLAS: No, madam, she will not dance with him, and I recommend you consider your words before speaking again about the prince's actions.

MARGARET: Mother, please...everyone is watching.

STEPMOTHER: *(Backing off.)* Very well.

ELINORA: Mother, are you alright? You frightened me.

STEPMOTHER: Yes, Elinora, dear. A wind just caught my dress.

MARGARET: I didn't feel any wind.

NICHOLAS: *(Calling him aside.)* Captain.

CAPTAIN: Yes, Sir Nicholas.

NICHOLAS: I suggest you keep a close eye on the three of them for the remainder of the evening.

CAPTAIN: Do you suspect some type of treasonous act, some sabotage?

NICHOLAS: I doubt that they are bright enough for that, but if they interrupt the prince and his lady friend, he will want both our heads.

CAPTAIN: Point well taken, sir.

NICHOLAS: Thank you, Captain.

SLOW FADE TO BLACK

SCENE 11

Coincidental Moments

At the Royal Garden Footbridge, just before midnight

SETTING: The Royal Garden Footbridge

AT RISE: The PRINCE stands on the palace side of the footbridge while CINDERELLA walks on the garden side. Her shoes are off and sitting at the foot of the bridge.

CINDERELLA: You really should try it, the grass is very soft. You would think my feet would be exhausted by now, especially in glass slippers.

PRINCE: Glass slippers?

CINDERELLA: Yes, they are quite remarkable. You should see them.

PRINCE: Oh, you're trying to trick me again. You know the deal.

CINDERELLA: Yes, Prince Henry.

PRINCE: Please, my lady, I've asked you to call me Henry.

CINDERELLA: Henry. I would never try to upset the nobility of what you are doing.

PRINCE: *(After a pause.)* Thank you, my lady, for dancing with me this evening. You turned a dreadful time into pure joy.

CINDERELLA: No, thank you. It has been the most memorable night of my life. I will always carry it with me.

PRINCE: *(Pauses again.)* It is time.

CINDERELLA: Time?

PRINCE: *(Trying to unknot his blindfold.)* Time to take this thing off. I should have done it the moment we met.

CINDERELLA: *(Quickly crossing the bridge and reaching up to stop his hands, she gets very close to him.)* No!

PRINCE: *(Pulling his hands away from the blindfold, he holds her hands around his shoulders.)* You're trembling.

(A lingering romantic moment as they lean closer for a kiss. But NICHOLAS enters suddenly, interrupting the kiss before it happens. THEODORE enters behind him.)

NICHOLAS: Your pardon, majesty.
PRINCE: Nicholas, what do you want?!
NICHOLAS: The...lady's coachman says he must speak with her. He is very insistent.
PRINCE: Very well.

(The PRINCE steps out of the light and talks to NICHOLAS in shadows on the side of the bridge that leads back to the castle. THEODORE pulls CINDERELLA over the bridge to the other side.)

THEODORE: My lady!
CINDERELLA: Theodore! I've had such a wonderful time. It's like the most amazing dream, I don't want it to ever end.
THEODORE: Cinderella, the time! It's nearly midnight!
CINDERELLA: Oh, I could dance until sunrise.
THEODORE: Cinderella, the magic will be gone at midnight! Remember? Your fairy godmother said that, at the stroke of midnight, everything will go back to the way it was before.
CINDERELLA: What?
THEODORE: You won't have horses and a carriage to take you home!
CINDERELLA: I would gladly walk home if only to spend just ten more minutes in his arms.
THEODORE: I will be a mouse again, Cinderella.
CINDERELLA: Oh, Theodore, I'm sorry. I've been behaving selfishly. You're right, we should go....I'm sorry you have to be a mouse again.
THEODORE: No, don't be sorry. I'm quite happy in my little mouse hole. This has been an exciting evening, but I'm ready to go back.
CINDERELLA: Let's go then.
THEODORE: Cinderella.
CINDERELLA: Yes, Theodore?
THEODORE: You've always been so kind to me. It has been an honor to be your coachman this evening, and to watch you these last few hours. To finally see true joy on your face and the sparkle of love in your eyes.
CINDERELLA: Love?

THEODORE: You should say goodbye.

(THEODORE walks further into the gardens. CINDERELLA crosses back to the PRINCE as he re-enters the light.)

CINDERELLA: Henry, I must leave you now.

PRINCE: But the night is young. Have I offended you in some way?

CINDERELLA: Oh, no! Not at all. I just can't stay any longer. Please try to understand.

PRINCE: *(Trying to unknot his blindfold.)* Very well, but I must see you first.

SFX: The first chime of the clock strikes. It slowly continues to chime 11 more times.

CINDERELLA: It's midnight!
PRINCE: Midnight already?
THEODORE: My lady, the time!
CINDERELLA: I have to go!
PRINCE: Just one moment.

(CINDERELLA runs up to the PRINCE in an attempt to get past him, but he is unknowingly blocking the end of the footbridge. She turns and runs toward THEODORE and into the garden.)

CINDERELLA: Goodbye!
PRINCE: Goodbye? Wait! Where are you going? Nicholas!
CINDERELLA: *(Realizing she left them at the bridge.)* Theodore, my slippers!
THEODORE: Go on, I will get them!

(CINDERELLA exits in a run.)

NICHOLAS: Yes, your highness?
PRINCE: Stop her, she's getting away!

(THEODORE picks up the slippers from the foot of the bridge as NICHOLAS crosses over to confront him.)

NICHOLAS: You! Stop there! You must take me to her!

(NICHOLAS pulls a slipper out of THEODORE's hand. He holds it up high as if to strike THEODORE. THEODORE squeaks like a scared mouse, pulls the glove off of his mouse hand and brings it up in a threatening gesture. NICHOLAS sees the monstrous hand, screams and runs into the PRINCE as THEODORE escapes into the garden with only one glass slipper.)

PRINCE: *(Finally getting his blindfold off, he struggles to focus his eyes.)* What happened? Where is she?

NICHOLAS: There was a monster!

PRINCE: What?

NICHOLAS: And...she got away, Henry.

PRINCE: No!

NICHOLAS: *(Handing him the glass slipper.)* She left only this.

PRINCE: She can't have gotten far. Follow her. Find her!

NICHOLAS: Yes, Your Highness.

(NICHOLAS runs into the garden.)

PRINCE: What have I done?! How could I let her get away? Find her!

BLACKOUT

SCENE 12

Tactical Errors

Balcony Seating, moments later.

SETTING: Cloud 8½ (or The Department of Minor Miracles and Blessings)

AT RISE: Clara and Mr. Richardson sit side-by-side, theater style. They are sharing a tub of movie popcorn.

CLARA: Oh, that stupid expiration timer of yours has ruined everything.
MR RICHARDSON: *(Disbelief)* She left the shoe.
CLARA: Well it's your own fault.
MR RICHARDSON: I can't believe she left the shoe.
CLARA: It's just one little glass slipper.
MR RICHARDSON: An enchanted glass slipper!
CLARA: Not anymore. Your ridiculous expiration timer has turned it back into an ugly old shoe by now.
MR RICHARDSON: No, Clara. The shoe must stay enchanted now because Prince Henry has it!
CLARA: I don't understand.
MR RICHARDSON: Don't you think he might get a bit suspicious if it suddenly changed into a dingy old shoe?
CLARA: Oh, right.
MR RICHARDSON: Right.
CLARA: Oh! Does that mean everything stays enchanted?
MR RICHARDSON: Just the dress and the shoes. She might still need them. Nothing else was directly connected to Cinderella so the enchantment ended on schedule.
CLARA: Does she get to keep the dress?
MR RICHARDSON: I'll allow it for one more day...until the stroke of midnight.
CLARA: Too bad. It's always nice when you get to keep the dress.

SLOW FADE TO BLACK

SCENE 13

Passion and Purpose

The Royal Palace Ballroom, 12:10 a.m.

SETTING: The Royal Palace Ballroom

AT RISE: The time on the palace clock is now 12:10. Music plays again at a low level. The King and Queen are dancing together. Attendants are cleaning up the room and the CAPTAIN stands at attention by the entrance.

PRINCE: *(Entering in a hurry. Out of breath.)* Father, call out the royal guard! I need our fastest horses!

KING: Calm down, Son.

PRINCE: No, Father, I won't calm down!

QUEEN: Sweetheart, why are you so upset?

PRINCE: She left, Mother! We were dancing and then she just left me!

QUEEN: It is late. All of the other guests have gone.

PRINCE: No, mother. She ran off.

KING: The beautiful girl you were with all night?

QUEEN: Why would she leave like that?

PRINCE: Was she pretty, Father?

KING: You didn't take the blindfold off?

PRINCE: No! I tried!

QUEEN: And you need the royal guard and the fastest horses to find her?

PRINCE: Yes, Mother...I-

QUEEN: You love her.

PRINCE: Yes.

KING: How is that possible? They just met. He's never even seen the girl.

QUEEN: Call the royal guard, Henry, and give our son your fastest horses.

CAPTAIN: *(Overhearing, he marches forward.)* Shall I assemble my men and prepare the horses, Your Highness?

KING: Make it so.

QUEEN: Thank you, Captain.

(NICHOLAS enters just as the CAPTAIN exits. NICHOLAS is out of breath and drops to his knees.)

NICHOLAS: I beg your forgiveness, Your Highnesses.
KING: What is it? What have you done?
PRINCE: Rise, Nicholas.

(NICHOLAS gets up off the floor and faces the prince.)

PRINCE: Tell me.
NICHOLAS: There is no sign of her. Not in any direction.
PRINCE: That can't be. She's a girl, not a ghost.
NICHOLAS: I caught up to her coachman, nearly had him in my grasp. I was looking right at him...and then he was gone. The gardens and the darkness just seemed to gobble him up. I searched the gardens, but in the darkness it was no use. I am sorry, Henry.
PRINCE: We ride tonight.
QUEEN: Where are you going?
PRINCE: Father, I still need your royal guard.
KING: Very well.
PRINCE: We will visit every house in the kingdom and try this slipper on the foot of every maiden.
QUEEN: Oh, sweetheart, you can't mean that. It could fit any number of girls.
PRINCE: I do mean it, Mother.
KING: Certainly this could wait until-
PRINCE: No, Father, it can't wait. Now that I've met her, I can't live another moment without her.
KING: I understand. You have my blessing, Son.
PRINCE: Thank you, Father. Come Nicholas!

(The PRINCE and NICHOLAS exit.)

QUEEN: Henry, what if he does something foolish?
KING: He's in love. Pray for him dear. Just pray.

SLOW FADE TO BLACK

[Start of optional mini scene to be played in front of the curtain during the scene change.]

> *(Three or more MAIDENs, including Cassandra, sit on the stage floor at a far end of the stage. They sit in somewhat un-ladylike, lamenting postures.)*

A MAIDEN: Why?!
A MAIDEN: Oh, stop whining. It's over.
A MAIDEN: I was so sure he was going to pick me. Now what are we supposed to do?
A MAIDEN: Go back to our dull, normal, boring lives. That's what.
A MAIDEN: Do you have any idea how much I spent for this dress!
A MAIDEN: My father mortgaged everything he owns to get me here. He's going to kill me when I come home without an engagement ring.
A MAIDEN: Me too!
A MAIDEN: I'm already engaged. My fiancé is going to kill me when he finds out I was even here.
A MAIDEN: Oh, that's bad.
A MAIDEN: How could any normal person afford a dress like that girl?
A MAIDEN: And glass slippers?!
A MAIDEN: Maybe she isn't a normal girl.
A MAIDEN: What?
A MAIDEN: Maybe she's royalty.
A MAIDEN: That's right! Maybe she's already a princess... from another kingdom!
A MAIDEN: She certainly looked like a princess.
A MAIDEN: Did anyone see her come in?
A MAIDEN: No.
A MAIDEN: I heard she snuck in through the royal gardens.
A MAIDEN: And she was never properly announced and presented to the royal court.
A MAIDEN: No one even knows her name.
A MAIDEN: What if this whole thing was just a ruse? A trick of some kind.

A MAIDEN: Sure! Why else would Prince Henry wear a blindfold? How could any of us stand a chance with him wearing that thing?

A MAIDEN: I think we were all deceived. None of us had a chance in the first place.

A MAIDEN: Do you really think so?

GUINEVERE: *(Suddenly entering and nearly rushing past them)* What are you all doing here?!

A MAIDEN: We think this whole thing was a charade. We've been duped!

GUINEVERE: Well I just heard that the mystery girl ran off.

A MAIDEN: What are you talking about?!

GUINEVERE: She bolted and Prince Henry is so crushed and desperate that he is going from house to house in search of a bride...tonight!

(The MAIDENs scream in delight/panic and rush to get off the floor and run out the exit at the opposite side of the stage. They ad lib lines like "I don't believe it.", "I've got to get home!", "My prince, my prince, come rescue me!", "But my hair has gone flat, I can't let him see me like this", "I'll never make it home in time", "I can't remember where I parked my carriage", etc.)

SLOW FADE TO BLACK

[End of optional mini scene section]

SCENE 14

Emergency Mission

Balcony Seating, moments later.

SETTING: Cloud 8½ (or The Department of Minor Miracles and Blessings)

AT RISE: CLARA and MR RICHARDSON still sit theater style. MR RICHARDSON loudly slurps through a straw in a large soda cup.

CLARA: Well you have certainly made a mess of things.
MR RICHARDSON: Me? What did I do?
CLARA: First you put an expiration timer on everything, which spoiled a wonderfully romantic moment. *(Dreamily)* He was about to look into her eyes-
MR RICHARDSON: *(After another loud slurp)* I spoiled a romantic moment?
CLARA: And then...true love's first kiss.
MR RICHARDSON: Oh, dear lord, I think she's lost it.
CLARA: And then you leave the enchantment on the glass slipper.
MR RICHARDSON: I had to do that.
CLARA: And now the prince is running around, waking up every young girl in the entire kingdom looking for a bride. Do you have any idea how many desperate young girls would be willing to cut off their big toe to fit into that slipper?
MR RICHARDSON: Are you suggesting some might try to deceive the prince? That a girl might try to trick him into thinking she was the one he danced with all night?

(CLARA crosses her arms and gives him a patronizing look.)

MR RICHARDSON: Oh my goodness.
CLARA: Now he gets it.
MR RICHARDSON: This could be very bad.
CLARA: I'm thinking we need another minor miracle.
MR RICHARDSON: The wand, please.

(She picks up the wand and hands it to him. He types along its edge.)

MR RICHARDSON: I'll take care of all the paperwork, you just get down there. Follow the royal guard, but stay out of sight this time. *(Handing the wand back to her.)* You know what to do.

CLARA: *(Saluting.)* Yes, sir.

BLACKOUT

SCENE 15

Revelation and Redemption

Stepmother's Kitchen, 1:30 a.m.

SETTING: Stepmother's Kitchen as before but the kitchen table is cleared.

AT RISE: Lights come up to an empty room.

(CINDERELLA enters, still in her ball gown and bare feet. She carries a glass slipper in one hand and has the other hand cupped against her waist holding THEODORE THE MOUSE. She crosses toward the fireplace, placing the glass slipper on the kitchen table as she passes.)

CINDERELLA: *(Gently moving cupped hands from her waist to the fireplace mantle.)* There you are, Theodore. Sleep well.

STEPMOTHER: *(Entering from the hallway, still in her ball gown. Behaving wickedly sweet.)* Cinderella.

CINDERELLA: Stepmother! I'm sorry did I wake you.

STEPMOTHER: Oh no, dear. I haven't been to bed.

CINDERELLA: Really?

STEPMOTHER: My goodness, Cinderella, isn't that a lovely dress. Wherever did you get it?

CINDERELLA: Oh this? It's...I-

STEPMOTHER: *(Picking up the glass slipper from the table.)* And what a beautiful glass slipper. How exquisite. But where is its mate?

CINDERELLA: I misplaced it.

STEPMOTHER: I'm sure it will turn up.

CINDERELLA: I don't know-

STEPMOTHER: Is there something you wanted to tell me, Cinderella?

CINDERELLA: Yes, Stepmother.

STEPMOTHER: Go on.

CINDERELLA: I was at the ball.

STEPMOTHER: *(Suddenly spiteful.)* Yes, Cinderella, I know you were at the ball. Do you take me for a fool?!

(JAMES appears from the gap at the fireplace.)

CINDERELLA: No, Stepmother.

STEPMOTHER: I recognized you immediately. I knew the prince would eventually see through your little masquerade and you would come crawling home. You were quite an embarrassment.

CINDERELLA: I don't understand.

STEPMOTHER: The way you danced the prince around for hours, manipulating him, toying with him. Everyone was talking about your disgraceful behavior. *(Yelling offstage.)* Margaret! Elinora!

CINDERELLA: No! That's not true!

JAMES: She's lied for so long she doesn't know what the truth is.

STEPMOTHER: You will not talk to me in this manner.

CINDERELLA: You are lying to me, Stepmother. You are jealous because Henry wanted to spend time with me and not your daughters.

STEPMOTHER: You take that back immediately!

CINDERELLA: No, Stepmother. I am not going to listen to you any longer. Not after tonight. You don't consider me one of your daughters and I don't think you ever have. I'm leaving here...I don't know where I will go, but anywhere else will be better than here.

(MARGARET and ELINORA enter from the hallway. They are also still in their ball gowns but are barefoot and somewhat "taken apart".)

MARGARET: I'm sorry, Mother, I tried to stay awake.

ELINORA: Me too...oh look who finally came home.

STEPMOTHER: *(Handing the glass slipper to one of the girls.)* Girls, Cinderella says she's leaving us, running away from home. Lock her in the cellar!

(THEODORE THE MOUSE appears from his hole on the mantle and starts running back and forth.)

CINDERELLA: What?! You can't!

JAMES: No, Evelyn, it doesn't have to be this way!

STEPMOTHER: *(She grabs the broom and holds it high to strike at the mouse.)* Well, if it isn't your little friend who always comes out when you need help.

(MARGARET and ELINORA grab CINDERELLA and force her out the hallway exit.)

CINDERELLA: Let go of me! Theodore, no! Get out of the way!

STEPMOTHER: Hold still you wretched little rodent.

JAMES: *(Pulling the broom out of her hands and putting it back against the wall.)* Stop!

(STEPMOTHER stares at the broom with a frightened look then looks jerkily around the room. THEODORE THE MOUSE runs back into his hole.)

JAMES: Killing a mouse won't make your pain go away.

STEPMOTHER: *(Fearfully.)* James? Is that you? James, darling?

JAMES: I'm here to help, try not to be afraid.

STEPMOTHER: Of course not. It's just my imagination.

JAMES: *(Walks behind STEPMOTHER and gently touches her shoulder.)* I just need to get your attention.

(STEPMOTHER spins around - still afraid but less than before.)

STEPMOTHER: *(Nervously talking to the air.)* It hasn't been easy you know! A widow with three little girls!

JAMES: You never forgave me for dying. Your anger is with me, not Ella.

STEPMOTHER: I don't know how it ended up this way. I never intended to make Cinderella a servant.

JAMES: It doesn't matter what you've done. What matters is what you choose to do next.

(MARGARET and ELINORA enter from the hallway.)

STEPMOTHER: You can't judge me, James. You haven't been here.

JAMES: I'm not judging you, Evelyn, I'm trying to help you.

MARGARET: Mother, are you alright?
STEPMOTHER: Oh girls, I'm so glad you're here.

SFX: Horse hooves.

(ELINORA crosses to the kitchen door.)

ELINORA: Mother, I believe it is the royal guard.
STEPMOTHER: Perhaps they are here to... arrest me.
ELINORA: Mother?
STEPMOTHER: Let them in.
ELINORA: Please come in, come in.
CAPTAIN: *(Stiffly entering with sword drawn at his shoulder in military procession style. Stands at attention throughout.)* His majesty, Prince Henry the Third.
STEPMOTHER: The prince?

(The PRINCE enters followed by NICHOLAS. NICHOLAS carries the glass slipper.)

PRINCE: Madam, I beg your pardon for the insensitive hour of my visit and for the lack of formal representation. But my mission is of the utmost urgency.
STEPMOTHER: Where is the fire, Prince Henry?
PRINCE: In my heart, madam.
STEPMOTHER: I see.
PRINCE: I ask that you present every eligible lady of the household, that she might try on this- *(NICHOLAS presents the slipper.)* glass slipper.
STEPMOTHER: A strange game for such an early hour of the morning. Wherever did you get such a lovely shoe?
PRINCE: It belongs to the girl I love, but I'm beginning to believe it may simply have fallen from the heavens. The girl whose foot it fits will surely be my bride.
MARGARET: Oh you found it, how wonderful! Where on earth did I leave it?
ELINORA: That's my slipper!
PRINCE: Ladies, if you would please just try it on. Then we will know.

(MARGARET sits down and NICHOLAS goes on one knee to assist her with the shoe. STEPMOTHER is distracted and slowly moving toward the hallway exit.)

JAMES: Evelyn, you can't leave her in the cellar. You must make the right choice this time.
MARGARET: It fits perfectly!
PRINCE: *(To NICHOLAS)* Wait for it.

SFX: Gunshot.

MARGARET: Ahhhhhhhh! Get it off! Get it off!

(NICHOLAS struggles but gets the shoe off of her foot. MARGARET and ELINORA trade positions.)

JAMES: *(Gently placing his hand on the side of STEPMOTHER's arm.)* You can do this. It's only a small step in the right direction, but it can open a new door.
STEPMOTHER: *(Gently rubbing her arm where his hand was.)* I don't think I realized until now just how much I missed you, James.

(She exits via the hallway and James follows her out.)

ELINORA: Gently!
NICHOLAS: Yes, my lady.
ELINORA: Be ready to take it right off!
NICHOLAS: Indeed, my lady.

(NICHOLAS helps ELINORA with the slipper.)

SFX: Gunshot.

ELINORA: Off! Take it off! Ahhhhhh!
NICHOLAS: *(Removing the shoe and then standing.)* Thank you ladies, for your time.
PRINCE: Are there no more eligible ladies of the house?
MARGARET: No, just the two of us.
PRINCE: Then we shall be off. Captain!

(CAPTAIN moves to open the door for the PRINCE.)

STEPMOTHER: *(Entering with CINDERELLA.)* Wait! What about Cinderella?
MARGARET: Mother, what are you doing?
ELINORA: She's lost her mind.
STEPMOTHER: Be quiet, girls. Come Cinderella, try on the slipper.

(CINDERELLA sits in the kitchen chair.)

NICHOLAS: *(Recognizing CINDERELLA.)* Henry, I think you should take this one.
PRINCE: Very well, I will humor you, Nicholas.

(The PRINCE goes on one knee, places the slipper on CINDERELLA's foot without even looking at her. He waits, ready for a scream.)

NICHOLAS: *(After a pause.)* If you are waiting for something to happen, it already has.
PRINCE: *(Finally looking up.)* It is you, isn't it? My lady with no name.
CINDERELLA: My name is Cinderella. Hopefully not the name of a wanted criminal.
PRINCE: Perhaps not a criminal, but very much wanted, I'm afraid.
CINDERELLA: And you with the eyes of a prince instead of a thief.
PRINCE: Why did you leave me in the garden?
CINDERELLA: I was afraid. I am not anymore.
STEPMOTHER: *(Handing him the other glass slipper.)* Your Highness, we really must keep the set together.
PRINCE: *(Putting the slipper on her other foot.)* May they never be apart again.
MARGARET: Mother, really! Do I mean nothing to you? Why would you let her out of the—
STEPMOTHER: Margaret, you don't understand.
PRINCE: Cinderella, if these ladies have hurt you in any way, my father's dungeon can accommodate them.
ELINORA: You and your big mouth, Margaret!

CINDERELLA: No, Henry. I hold no grudge against them. I never have. Just let them be.
PRINCE: As you wish.
CINDERELLA: Are you going to stay on that knee forever, Henry?
PRINCE: Only until you say you will be my bride. Tell me you will marry me today.
CINDERELLA: But Henry you still have fourteen days left.
PRINCE: I cannot bear even one more day without you at my side. Marry me today, Cinderella, and become my princess.
CINDERELLA: Yes, Henry, I will.

SLOW FADE TO BLACK

SCENE 16

Ripples and Waves

Mr. Richardson's Office, a moment later.

SETTING: The Department of Minor Miracles and Blessings

AT RISE: The desk is now covered with stacks of thickly stuffed file folders. MR RICHARDSON and CLARA stand at the edge of the scene looking down to earth. They are both sniffling from happy tears.

CLARA: Oh, it all worked out so beautifully.

MR RICHARDSON: Of course it worked out. It always works out. And it's clear now, why Cinderella's father was on special assignment.

CLARA: I don't suppose anyone else could have softened Evelyn's heart the way he did.

MR RICHARDSON: Yes, it all worked out quite nicely.

CLARA: But I have to admit, I was concerned.

MR RICHARDSON: Clara, I am the Manager of Coincidence Coordination.

CLARA: Well what does that have to do with anything? You didn't use any coincidences to help her.

MR RICHARDSON: No coincidences?! Madam, you insult my ability.

CLARA: I didn't mean-

MR RICHARDSON: I suppose you think it was just dumb luck that Cinderella and the prince shared their first moments together in the garden rather than the ballroom?

CLARA: Well I hadn't even considered-

MR RICHARDSON: I assure you, things might have worked out quite differently if they had not been allowed those quiet, romantic moments together.

CLARA: Yes, I suppose they might.

MR RICHARDSON: Clara, would you like to attend the wedding with me?

CLARA: Oh! That would be wonderful, sir!

MR RICHARDSON: Excellent! Then we ought to be going-

(They look back at the desk and see the stacks of papers and file folders.)

CLARA: Oh my goodness.

MR RICHARDSON: This is bigger than I expected.

CLARA: Where did all of it come from?

MR RICHARDSON: Related case files, reports, request forms-

CLARA: Related? To Cinderella?

MR RICHARDSON: *(Starts thumbing through random files.)* It would appear that way!

CLARA: I don't understand. I thought we were done.

MR RICHARDSON: *(Picks up a folder and fans its contents in a super speed read.)* The ripples, Clara. The ripples of a miracle always extend for hundreds and then thousands of years. Their great, great grandchildren, friends, loved ones — thousands of lives will be touched.

CLARA: I never imagined.

MR RICHARDSON: *(Fanning another folder.)* But this case appears to be very special!

CLARA: How?

MR RICHARDSON: *(Fanning another.)* It's the story. The fairytale. The minor miracles you bestowed on Cinderella will be interpreted as childhood fairy-magic, just as we intended.

CLARA: Oh, I'm sure she'll tell her children, and the grandchildren how they met and fell in love.

MR RICHARDSON: No, Clara, it's bigger than that. As the story is retold over time, it will transform into a popular fairytale. The story of Cinderella will touch millions, perhaps hundreds of millions of lives.

CLARA: But even if it grows into a mountain, it's still just a fairytale, sir.

MR RICHARDSON: *(Excitedly flipping through multiple folders.)* Children learning about hope and love through a simple fairytale. Lives being touched and changed by even the simplest versions of the story. The very name of Cinderella will become associated with a story of true love!

CLARA: There will be different versions?

MR RICHARDSON: The details, glass slippers, a fairy godmother-

CLARA: Oh my goodness, I'll be famous!

MR RICHARDSON: The details will change in each version. *(Picks up a very thick folder that he already scanned once.)* Here...Walt will tell it one way... *(Showing her a loose single piece of paper.)* But here's a Miracle Request form to inspire a version that even includes me.

CLARA: Mr. Richardson, you'll be famous too!

MR RICHARDSON: Yes, Clara, but my point is that the details may change, but the story of a girl who is pure of heart, finding true love — that's the ripple flowing through them all.

CLARA: I would never imagine a minor miracle having such impact.

MR RICHARDSON: Don't let the title fool you. There is never anything minor about the reach of a miracle. The term "minor" only refers to the size at its starting point. We didn't part the Red Sea, but- *(Gesturing to the piles of papers.)* -these ripples create a tidal wave of change.

CLARA: It's immense. Mr. Richardson, is there anything I can do to help you with all this?

MR RICHARDSON: Perhaps. Thank you for offering, Clara. But these can all wait until after the wedding.

CLARA: Oh that's right — it's this afternoon, isn't it?

MR RICHARDSON: Yes, it is. We need to get going.

CLARA: A royal wedding with only one day's notice. How can they pull that off? There are so many details to think about, something is bound to be forgotten.

MR RICHARDSON: I'm certain everything will be fine, Clara.

SLOW FADE TO BLACK

SCENE 17

Heaven Blessed

The Royal Palace Ballroom, 3:00 p.m.

SETTING: The Royal Palace Ballroom but without the thrones and Grand Ball settings. Instead, the room is decked out for a wedding.

AT RISE: Three clock chimes strike during the blackout and wedding processional music starts before the lights come up. The time on the palace clock is 3:00. The entire cast, including STEPMOTHER and stepsisters (but excluding THEODORE), is assembled for the wedding. The KING and QUEEN are on the groom's side with MR RICHARDSON and CLARA ("invisibly") on the bride's.

(Wedding Processional music is playing and the PRINCE enters when the lights come up. The PRINCE crosses to the groom's position.)

(A flower girl runs down the house aisle throwing rose petals.)

(CINDERELLA walks down a house aisle with JAMES at her side. However, they are not arm-in-arm as a bride and her father would normally be. Both her hands hold a bouquet of flowers and she walks in the center of the aisle as if she were alone. JAMES walks to the right of CINDERELLA with his left arm under her right forearm.)

(CINDERELLA pauses when she reaches the edge of the stage and turns with a look of doubt. JAMES gives her a gentle kiss on the cheek and moves to stand by CLARA. CINDERELLA touches her cheek and then proceeds up center to her waiting PRINCE as the processional music ends.)

CINDERELLA: Henry?
PRINCE: Shhh.
CINDERELLA: Henry, we've forgotten something.
PRINCE: As long as you are here, nothing else matters.
CINDERELLA: *(Indicating the empty spot where a minister should be standing.)* Henry, we have no one to marry us!

(Wedding guests gasp.)

MR RICHARDSON: *(Stepping into the minister's position.)* I believe I am qualified.
PRINCE: Sir, are you fully ordained?
MR RICHARDSON: By the very highest authority.
PRINCE: Then proceed!
MR RICHARDSON: Dearly beloved, we are gathered here in the sight of God-

(MR RICHARDSON continues the wedding in mime while the dialog continues. Main lighting dims and spot lighting focuses on the dialog. Lighting and vocal tones imply thoughts rather than spoken words of the characters.)

KING: Son, you have certainly done well. She is so beautiful.
CLARA: It's a match made in Heaven, Sire.
QUEEN: I do hope she will be a good mother.
CLARA: Oh don't worry about that. Three boys and four girls! It will be wonderful!

(The KING and QUEEN smile at each other and take each other's hand.)

JAMES: Shhh. Clara, the wedding.
CLARA: Oh, James, please. I have to talk; it keeps me from crying like a baby. Besides, they can't hear me any better than they can hear you.
JAMES: I've learned that there are times when they hear very well. Not our words-
CLARA: But they get the message, don't they?
JAMES: Yes. *(Pause)* Clara, try to get Ella to visit her stepmother occasionally. I know it may be difficult for her to look back, but Evelyn still has a long way to go.

CLARA: Oh, certainly. I'll do whatever I can to help. Perhaps you and I should have lunch together sometime, James. We could exchange notes.

(The general lighting comes back up as Wedding Recessional music starts)

MR RICHARDSON: -by the power vested in me from our Holy Father, I now pronounce Prince Henry and Princess Cinderella, husband and wife.

(The PRINCE kisses CINDERELLA as the cast applauds.)

(Recessional music fades to a low level under the dialog.)

PRINCE: *(Walking with CINDERELLA on his arm.)* I'll send Nicholas to get your personal things from your stepmother's house.
CINDERELLA: There's no need. I already brought everything I want in one small box.
PRINCE: One small box? What could that be?
CINDERELLA: A little friend of mine.

(They smile and exit together.)

CLARA: You know, Mr. Richardson, we didn't bring a wedding gift.
MR RICHARDSON: Oh alright, she can keep the dress.
CLARA: And the shoes?
MR RICHARDSON: Yes, Clara.
CLARA: Thank you, Mr. Richardson. You're such a softy.
MR RICHARDSON: You realize they will be keeping you a lot busier now?
CLARA: What do you mean?
MR RICHARDSON: You're the guardian angel for the whole family.
CLARA: Family? You mean when the children come, I'll be looking after all the little princes and princesses?
MR RICHARDSON: That's right.
CLARA: Oh my!

MR RICHARDSON: Don't worry. It will be easy with your new wings.

(CLARA brightens, smiles broadly and gives MR RICHARDSON a hug around the neck and a kiss on the cheek.)

BLACKOUT

The End

If you enjoyed *The Cinderella Miracle*, look for these other books and plays by Leonard Cary in the *Fairytales Happen... when angels make mistakes* series:

Beauty and the Beast's Betrayal

The Snow White Ambassador

The Aladdin Assignment

Sleeping Beauty's Intervention

SET PIECES & PROPERTIES BY SCENE

Scene 1: Desk, Two Chairs, Filing Cabinet (w/ folders & paper), 3x5 Card File (w/cards), Desk Telephone / Gold Pen, Pad of Paper, Clipboard, Five Stapled Paper Forms

Scene 2: Rustic Table, 1 or 2 Chairs / Mouse Puppet, Loaf of Bread, Thin Blanket, Broom

Scene 3: Scene 1 Set / Scene 1 Props

Scene 4: Scene 2 Set / Mouse Puppet, Captain's Sword, Royal Page's Scrolled Decree

Scene 5: Scene 1 Set / Scene 1 Props plus Handkerchief, Magic Wand, Approval Form

Scene 6: Scene 2 Set / Mouse Puppet, Needle & Thread, Scissors, Magic Wand, Theodore's Gloves (& Fur and black polish for his mouse hand), Dress & Shoes magic as detailed in the Production Kit, if desired.

Scene 7: Scene 1 Set / No Props

Scene 8: Two Thrones, Ballroom decor / Captain's Sash-Blindfold

Scene 9: Footbridge / Blindfold

Scene 10: Scene 8 Set / Scene 8 Props

Scene 11: Scene 9 Set / Scene 9 Props plus Glass Slippers

Scene 12: Scene 1 (or optional setting) / Move Popcorn Tub or Bag

Scene 13: Scene 8 Set / Scene 8 Props plus one Glass Slipper

Scene 14: Scene 1 (or optional setting) / Soda Cup, Magic Wand

Scene 15: Scene 2 Set / Mouse Puppet, Glass Slippers, Broom

Scene 16: Scene 1 Set / Large Stack of File Folders and Papers

Scene 17: Scene 8 Set minus Thrones plus wedding decor / Cinderella's Bridal Bouquet, Optional wedding items: Flower Girl Basket & Pedals, etc.

PRODUCTION KIT

Cloud 8 ½ Books offers an add-on enhancement to take your production of *The Cinderella Miracle* from ordinary to extraordinary. The kit includes the following set of tools:

Production Kit Manual
1. Illustrated steps to create the Scene 6 magic tricks and additional stage magic suggestions
2. Options and tips for "Theodore the Mouse"
3. Suggestions for scaling the show based on your budget, performance space and cast size
4. Other helpful production tools and tips

Music & Effects MP3s
A complete collection of music and sound effects created and licensed specifically for *The Cinderella Miracle*. Every sound effect referenced in the script is included and orchestral music includes an overture, scene changes, royal fanfares, grand ball waltzes, wedding procession/recession, and curtain call music.

Technical Cue Scripts
Seven copies of a specially formatted version of the script with all of the technical cues needed for most productions. Color coded lighting, sound, music and sound effect cues are already inserted at the correct points with plenty of room for changes to fit your production's needs. The scripts are in easy-to-read manuscript format and printed on 3-hole binder-ready pages that are 8 ½ x 11 single-sided to allow for facing-page note taking and readability during performances.

Please email info@Cloud8andahalfBooks.com at least 8 weeks in advance of your opening date for Production Kit pricing and ordering information.

SCENE 6 (Alternate Ending)

This is an alternate ending to Scene 6 if magic tricks will not be used. See the Production Kit for magic trick information. Note that the "Basket of clothing and linens" mentioned in the original setting is not needed if this ending is used. This alternate picks up from the following two lines of dialog in the original Scene 6.

CINDERELLA: Oh, please don't point that at me.
CLARA: But, Cinderella dear, you need a dress.
CINDERELLA: Well, not while I'm wearing it. That thing is dangerous.

(CINDERELLA begins to unzip her dress but turns to see THEODORE watching her.)

THEODORE: Is there something wrong, Cinderella?
CLARA: Oh really, dear, he's certainly seen you change before.
CINDERELLA: But he was just a mouse then. Could we go to another room?

(CINDERELLA and CLARA cross toward the hallway exit.)

CLARA: Certainly, dear, but we need to hurry. The clock is ticking and there is a deadline.
CINDERELLA: A deadline?
THEODORE: Don't forget, she'll need shoes to match.
CLARA: At the stroke of midnight, everything will go back to the way it was before.
CINDERELLA: Yes, I will need pretty shoes. I can't go in these.
CLARA: Leave that to me, dear. Go slip out of that dress. There's no time to waste.

(CINDERELLA exits via the hallway. CLARA stays back for a moment.)

CLARA: There is still so much to do, Theodore. We still need horses and a carriage with wheels.
JAMES: *(Appearing from the gap at the fireplace wall.)* Clara?
CLARA: Oh! Mr. Ashton, how nice of you to drop in.
THEODORE: Who are you talking to?

JAMES: Thank you, Clara. You are really making a difference this time. It means a lot to me.
CLARA: Oh, it is certainly my pleasure, Mr. Ashton. It means a lot to all of us.

(CLARA exits and THEODORE stays behind with a puzzled look on his face.)

SLOW FADE TO BLACK

Leonard Cary is a freelance author, playwright, composer, theater director, teacher, and professional computer software developer. He enjoys live theater and orchestral music, and has a bachelor's degree in trumpet and composition. He blogs at LeonardCary.com. His two adult sons were both homeschooled and are now making their own way in the world. But Leonard and his wife, Maggie, have little time to be empty-nesters because they continue to mentor homeschool students by staging theatrical productions, coaching a speech and debate team, and teaching enrichment classes that augment the educational opportunities and experiences of homeschooling families in the North Denver area of Colorado (CaryAnn.org).

Visit us at...
   Cloud8andaHalfBooks.com

www.ingramcontent.com/pod-product-compliance
Lightning Source LLC
Chambersburg PA
CBHW050543300426
44113CB00012B/2238